AF567145

THE BEEKEEPERS ANNUAL
IS PUBLISHED BY
NORTHERN BEE BOOKS
MYTHOLMROYD, WEST YORKSHIRE
& PRINTED BY
LIGHTNING SOURCE, UK
ISBN 978-1-904846-65-9

MMVIII

EDITOR, JOHN PHIPPS
NEOCHORI, 24024 AGIOS NIKOLAOS,
MESSINIAS, GREECE
EMAIL manifest@runbox.com

SET IN HELVETICA LT BY D&P Design and Print

Front Cover
Honeybee about to visit a sunflower -
but how much poison lies unseen within
its nectaries? *by John Phipps*

CONTENTS

FOREWORD

John Phipps

October 2010

Whilst writing this Foreword I am reminded of the enormous debt that The Beekeepers Quarterly owes to this publication which started way back in 1983. In order to keep beekeepers up-to-date with any changes to the diary section in particular, two Supplements were produced, which in turn led to the creation of The Beekeepers Quarterly. With the BKQ reaching its 100th issue this year, it was a good time to look back over the last quarter of a century and to see how beekeeping has changed during that time - though sadly, not for the better. Numerous problems face beekeeping in the UK today and there are other threats on the horizon which might have to be faced in the near future, especially as regards yet more exotic pests and diseases. However, as in the past, and hopefully in the years to come, there will be beekeepers who are alert to any changing situation and, through the pages of both The Annual and The Beekeepers Quarterly, will be able to give up-to-date news on what is happening and how problems might be solved.

In the 100th issue of The Beekeepers Quarterly many of our past writers reflected on the last twenty-five years of beekeeping - and in memory of those who are no longer with us, we are remembering them in the 2011 Annual by republishing a selection of their articles as a tribute to their long service with us.

For those beekeepers who are new to the craft, back issues of The Beekeepers Quarterly are still available which contain excellent advice from some of the world's top ranking beekeepers.

Lets hope that 2011 is a good year for us all.

John Phipps

THE CHURCH AND THE BEEKEEPER

John Kinross

This is the time of Easter and also the time to write up the notes of the annual spring meeting of the TARANOV Board (Tomes and Reprints Absolutely Not on Varroa) at our local pub. Ina Strainer has always been a lazy beekeeper and she was delighted with "How to Keep Bees Without Finding the Queen" by Paul Mann (NBB £6.50). The book has useful mini-nuc construction plans but no index which is a pity thought the Professor who says he always makes his own with red ink.

From IBRA comes Dorothy Hodges "Pollen Grain Drawings"

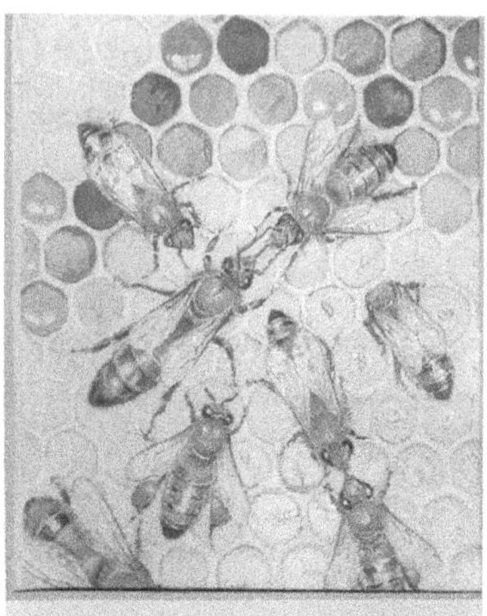

(£5.50) which can be useful for microscope addicts. Ina says that the last walnut cake she made came out like a picture of Greater Bindweed pollen and the Marrow, to my mind, looks like a mine washed up on Charlestown beach when we lived there.

For bumblebee enthusiasts there is the new edition of Goulson's "Bumblebees, behaviour, ecology, and conservation" (£29.95) which has some fine colour illustrations in the centre. From Collins comes the vast "Beekeeper's Bible" (£30) which includes everything - recipes, carrying beehives in Greece (the Professor says that the picture could be him as he worked in a Greek monastery one summer, but Ina says that the picture of the Aboriginee is more like him). It is quite a tome that will no doubt prop up quite a few beekeeper's library shelves.

Book of the year award goes though to NBB for their excellent production "Beekeeping for All" by Abbe Warre (£11) which has been translated from the French by the Heafs from North Wales. The Abbe had time and patience to design and produce his own hive during the last war (he died in 1951) so he called it the "People's Hive" and it was very popular in France. The Abbe dressed up in his long black robes and broad hat for his bees - though Brother Adam always wore a veil.

It is surprising how many clergymen wrote bee books in their spare time and experimented with different hives.

Edward Beavan was one and in Kilpeck church I found a tombstone to the Rev E Beavan and his wife Phillippa.

Just before writing this, we had our Beekeeping AGM in the WRVS hall. I arrived early to see that the church group had beaten us to it and a young cleric was setting up a screen. They moved down the corridor without a problem. However, during the next twenty minutes about a score of people arrived, some beekeepers, some church goers, some both. We really could have combined the two meetings as our president is a lay reader and his report reads a bit like a sermon. Personally, I think all beekeepers need to pray for the survival of their bees and that there will always be a close affinity between church and bee folk.

The story for the Annual this year is an island story. On many Scottish Islands the able-bodied have more than one job and in Orkney recently there was a flu scare so all the population was injected. The queue went all round the health centre bungalow. My friend was near the end. Suddenly the man in front went down on all fours. "Why are you doing this?" asked my friend. "Get down", he replied. "Dr MacDonald has gone to open the chemist's, so we have Percy instead." "So, who is Percy?" enquired my friend. "Percy Reid - he is the vet from Westray - if you don't go in on all fours he won't know where anything is!"

BROTHER ADAM, 3RD AUGUST 1898 - 1ST SEPTEMBER 1996.

WELL-BRED QUEENS

Brother Adam

Young, well-bred, vigorous queens are the *sine qua non* success in beekeeping. There exists no surer, more certain safeguard against disease and the numerous minor troubles of apiculture. Old or poorly bred queens will not only fail to produce healthy, vigorous stocks - the kind required for obtaining the maximum surplus per hive — but their degenerate progeny are susceptible to every malady bees are subject to.

Paradoxical as it may seem, the majority of beekeepers fail to take the simplest and most essential precaution of keeping their apiaries free from disease. Of course, no one depending on bees for his livelihood would venture to keep a large number of stocks without re-queening them annually.

I stated that young, well-bred, vigorous queens are the bedrock to success in beekeeping. Obviously every queen reared is young, but not necessarily well-bred and vigorous — a distinction of paramount importance. It is the easiest thing in the world to rear queens, but to rear the very best, queens that are long-lived, full of vigour and stamina, and rear such in changing seasons and weather is a task demanding exceptional skill, experience and constant vigilance. There is, however, one method by means of which the merest

novice is enabled to raise excellent queens.

A stock suitable for raising cells by this method must cover no less than twenty B.S. combs.

First and foremost the bees must be in a condition to elaborate royal jelly in abundance. This they are only in condition to do during a light honey flow; or when no nectar is available feeding of diluted honey in liberal quantities, approximately three to four pints per day, is resorted to. If feeding is required it must commence five days prior to the time a colony is expected to start cell building. The object is to turn all the energies of the chosen colony to the building of queen cells.

This is achieved by making it queenless and entirely broodless. The two brood chambers containing the whole colony are removed from the hive and one empty brood box placed in position on the floorboard instead. The queen is now first found and caged, then nine combs containing honey and pollen, but no brood or eggs whatever, are placed into the empty brood chamber and one comb of eggs of the breeding queen. All the bees on the combs of brood are then shaken or brushed back into the hive. The bees deprived of queen and brood will commence building queen cells within a few hours and in five days hence the cells will be sealed. As soon as the cells are completed the queen and brood, which meanwhile were placed on top of a strong stock, are now returned. A queen excluder must of course be placed between the brood chamber containing the fertile queen and the newly sealed cells. On the eleventh day from the time the cells were commenced the virgin queens are due to hatch.

The supreme advantage of this method of raising cells consists in that the royal larvae receive a superabundance of chyle from the very moment the eggs hatch. Queen cells built under the supersedure impulse, in a queenright colony, above an excluder, are very often indifferently cared for.

From The Beekeepers Quarterly, No 47, Autumn 1996.

BERNARD MOBUS

TRAVELLERS' TALES

Bernard Mobus

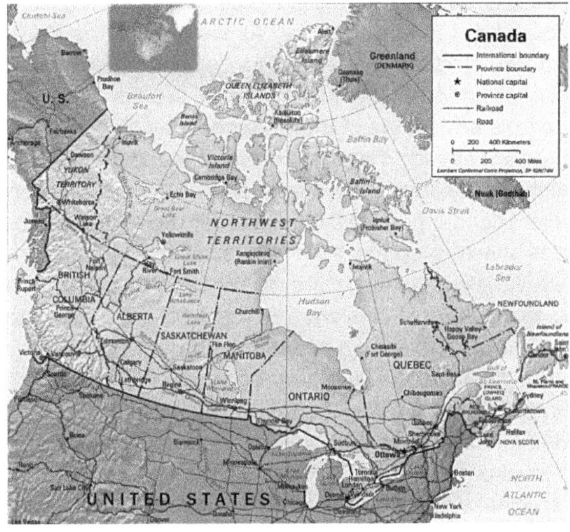

Canada is a country I visited recently. It is a vast place, of course, but one rarely realises the fact until one has travelled about a bit. We landed at Calgary and hired a car to see the Rockies, a part of the prairies, the range lands of the Western Provinces before going on to relatives on Vancouver Island. We did not fail to visit some beekeepers on our trip, of course.

After the journey through the Banff and Jasper National Parks with their impressive scenery, we turned north through the Prairies of the Peace River area and called on a beekeeper who had settled in Canada some 30 years ago. He had learned beekeeping at home but had to change and adapt to the new conditions of long and severe winters. At first he built up to 500 colonies and 'worked' them extensively, which means that colonies hardly got any attention at all. This gave him time to attend to farm work as well, although yields per colony suffered. When winter came he killed all stocks as did all other beekeepers in that part of the world, and he bought in more packages each spring from California. He reduced the number of stocks when packages became more and more expensive and payed more attention to his colonies at the same time. As the prices for packages rose further, he began to experiment with overwintering colonies in special bee-houses, just as he had been used to in Austria.

By studying his failures with an enquiring mind he improved his wintering sheds for colonies with heavy insulation and artificial heating to make stocks survive even better. In the end he found that by manipulating humidity as well as temperature and by providing stimulating feeds of syrup, pollen and water after January, he could shake out several 'packages' by late April and just buy a fresh queen for each. His best total honey harvest from one colony and the shaken packages from it amounted to 1 500 1b of honey in one season. This past summer season had been a bad one in Canada (due to drought) and his overall honey take had been down considerably and had amounted to only 1701b per colony! Because of other commitments, he runs a 360 acre farm and is Canada's National Olympic team coach for luger (sledging), he has reduced the number of his stocks considerably.

Large stands of willows among aspen and poplars provide early pollen and at times even a honey surplus from forward stocks. As we walked the fields we discovered that between the dry grasses there was a dense stand of green and deep rooting dandelions. In spring these flowers can fill supers when the stocks are strong enough to take advantage of them. Dandelions give a yellow honey with a strong but pleasant flavour. The main crop of beekeepers in his area consists of honey from rape followed by alfalfa and clover. Goldenrod and fall aster, a kind of wild Michaelmas daisy, help to fill brood boxes for the winter. The oilseed rape there is spring sown because the winters are too severe for autumn sown varieties. When this crop comes into flower, the colonies are stronger and temperatures are warmer, and so the Canadian beekeepers do not have the same problem we experience here in Britain with OSR. Besides, by then other sources are available and a blend of nectars does not show the pronounced tendency to granulate.

We then went on to Beaverlodge, the Agricultural Research Station in Alberta, and called on the Beekeeping Unit. Dr. Tibor Szabo was out on that day but Dr. Liu showed us around. We were shown the way they survey cluster and hive temperatures of wintering colonies and other work done on improving wintering in the severe climate. Temperatures drop below freezing for many months and can fall below -40°C (-40°F) frequently. At the Research Station all hives are now placed in groups of four before winter comes. Insulating blankets of plastic sheets, interspaced with fibre-glass all around, are used to improve wintering and the packs are provisioned with top entrances for additional ventilation and chances of flight. Packing is done - late November and when the two story colonies have at least 801b of winter stores. Dr. Liu is the honeybee pathology expert and requested our help in obtaining samples of bees with an infection of acarine disease. Scottish bees and mites are now in his hands and will be used for a study of the damage to tissues by means of X-ray scanning electron microscopy. The problem of acarine disease has now come to the beekeepers of the Americas; but that was reported in another issue already.

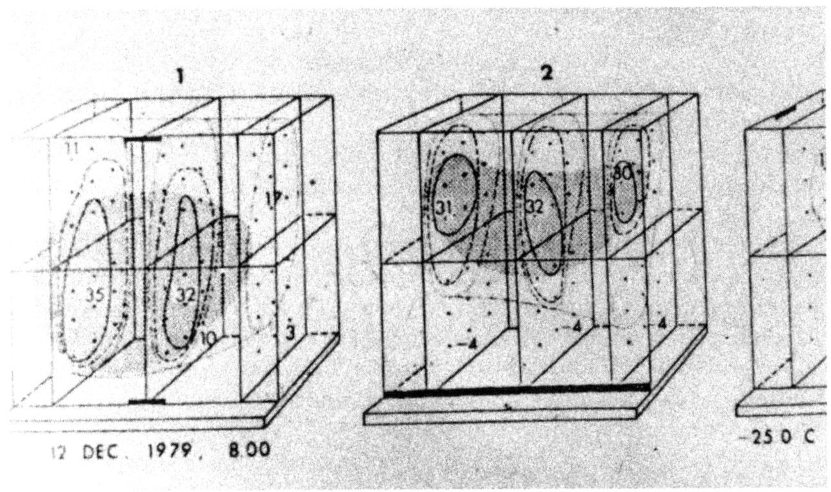

A COMPUTER IS USED TO CREATE 3D IMAGES OF CLOUDS OF TEMPERATURES ABOVE 30C (86 DEGREES F).

'Doing Canada' by driving 2000 miles in 8 days leaves you with little time for detailed study of beekeeping. I would have liked to have visited the township of Falher which claims to be the 'Honey Capital' of the Prairies. It is said that here along you can find 30,000 colonies, or probably the same number of hives as in the whole of Scotland. That journey would have meant another 300 miles and another two night's car hire and stay in motels. We heard also about one beekeeper who fastens plywood floors firmly and leak-proof to his hives, tilts all hives backwards in autumn and simply pours in the sugar syrup until

it flows out of the front door! The syrup rises between honey combs and few bees drown. It is then stored in the upper combs for winter feed. After returning the hired car we flew on to Vancouver Island for a family visit. But which beekeeper can leave it at that? So, not surprisingly, we investigated beekeeping there too. Joanne found one apiary and I investigated. That beekeeper was using the Langstroth hive like everybody else, but he had adopted the shallower frame (Dadant shallow) as a basic unit for broad and honey production. Honey had been harvested by the time we arrived and the bees were ready for winter, which is much milder on the island than in the rest of Canada. Some bees were of pure Italian strain and a few were mongrels showing some black (Carniolans are preferred for 'hybridising'). The pure Italians had spread out on the crown board underneath the roof on a wonderfully fine day, but all migrated slowly back to the feed-hole and the warmth of the colony. Yet the air was quite warm and our type of bees would have been 'happy' to fly and collect nectar and pollen from the still plentiful hawksbeard (an 'autumn dandelion' for want of a better description) and fall aster.

Some hive parts were strewn around negligently and I discovered that a very interesting part of the owner's beekeeping, and apparently favoured in many parts of Canada, was the 'Killion' board which is placed over the floor board. In this apiary it was even used to restrict a weaker colony to a single brood box and to isolate the unoccupied boxes by means of this board. It is a slatted floor and consists of a spacer frame with 2" laths, leaving a beeway-sized gap between them. The slatted floor adds space below the frames and improves ventilation here without letting bees extend their combs. Carl Killion is credited with this invention and he used it extensively when working crowded stocks for section production.

The owner of the out-apiary was away on holiday, but the neighbouring chicken farmer (he runs a small outfit of 14,000 hens on his own) helped me trace a beekeeper in Victoria through the Yellow Pages and we visited Babe's Honey Farm the following day. Babe Warren is the boss and Charlie is permitted to call himself that when his wife is not around. Both are 68 and very active still. Honey extracting was still in progress and three parallel-radials, each with a 120 frame capacity were waiting for more supers to come in. All extractors are loaded directly from one mobile uncapping machine. In the warehouse we saw stacks of empty supers which would have been a credit to any Texan: they were vast and could hold two banks of 25 frames each. Some were of full Langstroth depth for 9" frames, others were for Dadant or Langstroth shallows. When you think of 50 Langstroth deep frames full of honey, (the equivalent of 5 broad boxes or 2501bs of honey alone), you realise that Canadian beekeepers must be strong and possibly originate from the tribe of the 'Big Foot', a mythological Yankee-doodle-Yeti of the Rockies (with a yodel of 'Alouette', of course).

The answer to the question of large supers was soon discovered. Charlie had experienced so much damage by bears in his apiaries, and this location needed so much expensive electric fencing, that he decided to try another tack. He fastened 10 Langstroth hives - 2 rows of five - to one pallet and covered all of them with one large roof. The block would be a 'colony' too large even for a strong grizzly to turn over and vandalise and would be safe without fencing. Then he decided to make his super so large, that two supers would easily cover the ten colonies on one pallet. Mechanised lifting equipment, such as we find it on lorries handling timber and brick pallets nowadays, make it easy to shift whole apiaries in no time at all or to lift supers up when inspections demand this. All hives on pallets are excluded without fail in order to avoid queen losses, although hives in single units received no excluder in his management. Worker bees can mix freely in the supers once they have been placed on hives in late spring.

Snags? It appears that duff or failing queens are not superseded as readily in this system because the queen substance from all queens is available throughout for even distribution. Good beekeeping and keen observation must bring about artificially what nature would look after through supersedure under normal circumstances. He would therefore now turn to queen rearing from his best stocks as a means of having spare queens for introduction where they are needed. Similarly, mating flights from colonies in a block are occasionally unsuccessful when returning virgins go to the wrong front door at a busy time so small queen rearing nucs are always at hand to remedy any problem. Removing supers is another problem which had to be solved in an old fashioned way. The long distances involved between apiaries - he travels 250 miles to his furthest out-apiary, - and his large supers and hives would make clearer boards inefficient and costly. His large supers are even too cumbersome for efficient use of blowers. He has gone back to the old carbolic cloth to drive bees from supers and saves time and extra journeys that way.

His main flow is from fireweed or rosebay willowherb with other wild and moorland flowers making a contribution. He even is convinced that our native broom, which came to Vancouver Island as ballast or packing as an importation, can produce nectar in sometimes copious quantities.

Flying home, we noticed that the fall colours of golden leaves on aspen, poplars and birch had been blown off the trees and that a thin blanket of snow was covering the area around Calgary. In Britain the trees were still green and in full leaf. Bees had been winter-fed in the traditional, old fashioned way and were also ready to face the next few months ahead.

From The Beekeepers Quarterly No 7, Autumn 1986.

IS BRITAIN'S WEATHER CHANGING? PERHAPS WE SHOULD ASK THE BEES!

Bill Clarke
Cambridge
Spring 2010

I have been having a clear-out - again! Interesting finds turned an hour's job into all day. Some yellowing pages surfaced, copied from Cambridge BKA Newsletters, linking the weather, state of the bees and honey yields during 1915 to 1938, which I had hoped to use when I was Editor. Can I bring it up to date? Our changing times - and beekeepers - have moved the emphasis away from earliest/biggest swarms, number of supers or weight of honey to more academic enlightenment, certainly a plethora of methods to just keeping the bees alive. Clues are there, weather certainly, and I know if it is a swarmy year as the phone never stops; nevertheless, I had to widen my search, and deciding to go for a century made it more difficult but interesting! However, I couldn't resist this in Richard Mabey's booklet, 'Cold Comforts' for: "April 23rd - 26th 1908, 12 inches of snow lay in parts of Norfolk and Suffolk," so let's make it 101 years!

1909**, British Bee Journal** Aug 11th**:** "The Mammoth Show at Cambridge is fast becoming known as the best show in the United Kingdom...despite the fact that owing to the bad weather many large exhibitors were unable to show." 1910: **BBJ** Aug 10th. Glamorgan B.K.A. Annual Show: "competitors were representative of all parts of the country. The season has been unusually favourable, etc." My pencil research had reached the 1990s, when my wife pointed out a book that I had missed - **The Agricultural Records, (AR) A.D. 220 to 1977**, by J M Stratton; he says of 1910: "A rather wet cloudy summer, but with very good crops," goes on to mention frost and snow in January, then rain, cool, dull, storms, very little sun, all taking turn and turn about, except for "a warm and summer-like June", finishing with "December, wet and mild". Has he thrown a spanner in the works? No. This was the only year that he seemed to be at odds with the bees. I believe 1910 was one of those years when the short periods of sun coincided with the main flowering times.

Next, I had just arrived at this point in my typing when I was given a box of beekeeping literature by BBC Radio Cambridgeshire presenter Christopher South, from his 102 year-old uncle, Len Beyton, who had just gone into a care home. As I rifled through Ministry leaflets, I discovered No 5, by the **Village Bee Breeders Association for 1967 - VBBA - entitled, Bees, Honey and Weather**, which has helped fill some holes, starting with 1911: "said to be the best of all time," - and show that I am not the first to make the link! 1912, **Cold Comforts** states: "August 25th to 26th, severe floods in East Anglia. In Norwich 7.3 inches (178.6 mm) of rain fell in less than 24 hours, and the River Wensum raced through the city, destroying almost all the bridges." The **AR** for 1913 records a dull year but: a very dry summer which was, however, neither sunny nor warm," and for 1914; "a mild sunny year." With the horrendous war - and the bees suffering a build up of disease starting in 1910 on the Isle of Wight - it is not surprising there is little mention of honey yields except for Harrison Ashforth reporting on past seasons in a **1984 BBJ**: "1915 V.G. season in South and West. Poor in North." For 1916 - the year that many thought British beekeeping was about to be eliminated, **AR** records: "A dull wet year," and for 1917: "A cold year with a wet summer." **Cold Comforts** mentions June 28th for the "Heaviest Rainfall in one day of 9.56 inches (242.6 mm) in Bruton, Somerset," and the **VBBA** puts 1917 in their list of bad honey years. **AR** gives 1918 as "Rather wet," and 1919 as "Generally dry."

1920 **AR** records as: "A dull year, with a cool damp harvest." **VBBA**, lists July 1921 as "rather warm and sunny, a good honey year". For 1922 the **CBKA** reports poor weather, finally resulting in starving colonies and the **VBBA** puts it in their bad year list, the **CBKA** reports 1922, 23 and 24 as very similar - except for 1923 having "a hot end to June into July", and 1924 giving an average honey yield of 30-40 lbs (9-18 kg) only for those whose bees were on the chalk, visiting sainfoin and white clover. 1925 was a poor spring in Cambridge, resulting in many colony losses, but **H Ashforth** reported: "V.V.G. honey season." The 1926 Cambridge spring "caused the apple crop to fail, but the honey yield was similar to 1924. **R. O. B. Manley mentions**

1927 in his book, Bee-Keeping in Britain: "in this locality - Benson Oxfordshire - the worst any beekeeper could remember," and the **CBKA** reports: "Worst season for 50 years generally." Their 'Expert', suggested the heavy losses had much to do with the type of bees, the English bee was very quick to throw out drones and drone brood in a food shortage, even throwing out worker grubs if things got very tight; whilst the Italians from a climate of double harvests didn't have the habit. **Manley** next reports that 1928 was one of the best seasons he ever had, however, he was disappointed because he had lost many colonies in the previous poor season and hard winter. In 1929 the Cambridge bees fared well - gaining from an early flow from the charlock, to give a local average of 50 lbs (22.5 kg) and some over 200 lbs (90.7 kg).

1930: **Manley** writes: "I cannot remember two very bad years coming together until 1930 and 1931." **AR** has 1932 as: "Another dull year, with little sunshine." The **CBKA** report "very trying weather for 1933, but the lucky ones near the charlock and clover, getting as much as 230 lbs, 104.3 kg per hive, although late drought meant that some lost their early gain. For **Manley** and much of the country, it was a very good season. The **CBKA** report 1934 "starting well, then an early June drought causing much starvation". 1935 was described as: "Icy May followed by depressing June and then a prolonged drought - the worst season for many years," unusually, finishing with: "Cambridgeshire worse off than other parts." In 1936 they blame a lack of sun countrywide for 10 lb (4.5 kg) honey yields, but Cambridge had an average of 25 lbs (11.3 kg). 1937 was also poor countrywide, with many winter losses due to lack of feed; however lucky CBKA members near second cut red clover - which flowered during the one hot spell in August - averaged 50 to100 lbs (22.6 to 45.3 kg). 1938 saw March leap into summer, with bees filling sections from early blossom; then April plunged back to winter, cutting all the blossom - even quite tight buds, the sainfoin and the limes. Three months of drought followed, and most districts had little honey to harvest.

There is a lack of literature for the war years - amazingly, perhaps showing the resolution of beekeepers - the Cambridge Expert still went to the International Congress in Zurich in August 1939, even inviting Dr Matilde Hertz back to speak at the CBKA AGM! **Manley** reports that heavy colony losses for the 1939 and 1940 winters, can be blamed on the prevalence of acarine, and the **VBBA** leaflet puts the 1940 summer as above average for sunshine, with good honey yields. **AR** gives 1941 as: "A dull cool year on the whole," whilst **Manley** mentions 1942 as a year when a lovely hot June failed to deliver a honey crop - he blamed it on exceptionally cold and dry east winds right through May and early June. 1943 is my own first memory of a good honey crop - which I hope was countrywide, although **AR** puts it as: "A mild wet year on the whole." - Aged 11, I was engaged to spin out the honey at an apiary in Bedfordshire. I well remember the angry bees, and the apiarist being ecstatic at the finish, saying that we had averaged over 100 lbs, 45.3 kg per hive. **AR** gives 1944 as: "A dull year with an unsettled summer." **H Ashforth** rated 1945 as very good in the North and Midlands, whilst **Manley** rates it as, "Bad". **The Good Bee-Keeping** (**GBK**) magazine for July 1946 carried a notice from the Ministry of Food: "Because of the exceptionally bad weather, sugar has been made available for feeding the bees." 1947 was the year which one Newspaper recently described as, "The awe inspiring winter," snow remained into late spring, yet there were the highest honey yields since 1928. In August 1948 the **GBK** magazine reported: "The honey season at the time of writing has been a complete failure in all parts of Britain, with many cases of starvation on the heather moors." To end the 1940s, a **Norfolk BKA Newsletter** quotes: "1949 for most parts has been good, giving surpluses of over 100 lbs (45.3 kg) - with many places in south west England having yields of over 200 lbs (90.7 kg)."

My 1950s **Cambridge Newsletters** - up until today - are fairly complete, but weather and honey news is scarce. The first clue that the 1950s and 1960s were not all honey and roses, is in the **VBBA** leaflet, Table 2, 'Comparison with the pre-war ten years up to 1937.' For the average accumulated temperatures in degree days above 60 degrees F for England and Wales: there were 50 days less per year for the ten years ending at 1956, and 87 days less per year for the ten to 1966. And also quoted is the average honey yield of 46 lbs, 20.8 kg per colony before 1936, dropping each of the next ten years, through 42, 19 kg, 39, 17.6 kg,and 30, 13.6 kg, for the last ten to 1966. My first thought was that the rise in arable farming coupled with better weed suppression - no more honey crops from charlock is just one instance - could also have been responsible for the lower honey yields; however **Beowulf Cooper** does take account of this. This decline in honey yield also follows closely the removal of the British Black bee from the gene pool. **Beowulf** mentions visiting a Cambridgeshire fruit farmer in 1950, who complained that he wasn't getting good pollination from his hired bees. It was a cool, windy day, and a Norfolk Bee-farmer's black bees were working apple blossom assiduously, whilst Italian hybrids- with bigger populations in the hives- stayed at home. Elsewhere in the leaflet he mentions that there is a 10 degrees F difference in temperature, between when the black bees and the light coloured hybrids venture out, but even when factoring in these anomalies, the relationship between good weather and honey gathering was little changed. There is little nectar flow in cold temperatures anyway. The titles of 'Times' articles used by the **AR**, are all we need to wrap up the 1960s: "RAINFALL IN 1967 GREATER THAN AVERAGE FOR THE THIRD CONSECUTIVE YEAR," 1968 SUMMER WAS WETTEST SINCE 1931," "RAINFALL UP AGAIN IN ENGLAND," for 1969.

1970 and **AR** continues much the same, but mentions a long dry spell in the middle for many areas. For 1971 the **CBKA Circular** Editor writes: "On the whole we can say that so far it has been a fair season," sadly, 'A Beeman', in a 1972 **Circular** follows with: "... so far this has been just about one of the worst seasons in memory!" The Editorial for the 1974 **Circular** was nearly as gloomy: "This summer has continued to test our tempers. Early May brought a heavy blow ... wet weeks that followed, reduced the hives to a minimum of stores." Spirits lifted in 1975: "Despite a drought from mid-May to mid-December, many members had the best year they can remember." A friend of the Editor of **BeeCraft** remarked, as he looked at the parched earth "They are sucking it out of the stones!" However, a worse drought, coupled with heat, was to come in 1976 -it is certainly built in to my own memory, by the loss of hundreds of mature trees on the estate I managed - yet the **CBKA** Editor writes: "... rarely less than 40 lbs (18 kg), many up to 80 lbs (36 kg), and some well above that ... how anything flows at this juncture, etc." Having come to the end of the **AR**, I now have to rely on **Jeff Rounce** and his comments in the **British Bee Journal (BBJ)**. He mentions that 1977 had been an odd year, but that he did take between 30 and 35 lbs (13.6-15.8 kg). For 1978 he complained that: "I have had the worst year for eight years with an average yield of 19 lbs (8.6 kg)" saying it seemed to be countrywide. 1979: **Jeff** had more cause to complain, the wet right through to April resulted in limited honey from his orchard contracts, but he got a little from the oil seed rape - unfortunately he had lost 7% of his colonies during the previous winter and a quarter of the remainder were in no state to gather a surplus. In fact it was the result of that winter and the following cold wet spring destroying all the wild honeybees on my estate that made me decide to take up beekeeping.

1980: **Jeff** is writing in August that despite having to feed bees, and wondering if his third bad season is in the offing, things had picked up and he expected to take an average of nearly 30 lbs (13.6 kg). The **CBKA**, Apiary Manager writes in the **1981 Yearbook**: "the meetings had been badly affected by the poor weather," and in the 1982 **BBJ** December Editorial, Cecil Tonsley says: "After a winter of some of the severest weather experienced this century, May gave promise of a really great honey year ... June did not fulfil its role ... surely by the last of June . . . change for the better ... nothing of the sort happened . . . apart from those in Oil Seed Rape growing districts, many colonies were starving," and finished with: "a good flow from the ivy, after all the bees had been fed!" 1983: **Jeff** writes in October, "on the last day of June the weather relented ... The net result has been a better than average season;" and in December he admits to: "... having my best season since 1976." The **BBJ** Editorial for October 1984, hints at a mixed year, with some areas having a bumper season, others grumbling that drought reduced their take. Little is said anywhere about the 1985 honey crop, except in the **BBJ** under, 'CORNWALL CALLING!': "As expected honey yields are well down ..."

ending with, "... around half of an average season's yield." The 1986 spring revealed colony losses of 25 - 30%, only for more miserable weather to see off further colonies. The amateur weatherman tried to lift spirits, predicting a long hot summer, but it only picked up enough to allow apiarists to make up colony numbers - not sell honey! 1987 started very cold and and snowy - again the amateur weatherman predicted the longed for summer - however **Jeff** had this to say in November: "The least said about 1987 the better, except that three poor seasons in a row is unusual." 'Beelines' in **Thorne's Beekeepers News** wrote of 1988: "... a record year for us, but one cannot say the same for honey yields. As always, some beekeepers report bumper yields from one apiary but from another, probably only a few miles away, practically nothing." For me at Wandlebury, 1989, the only year I managed to find time to keep nine hives, was THE honey year - nearly half a ton - 490 kg. It seems to have been countrywide, 'AIREDALE' in his **BBJ** column for December, writes: "This golden year has seen plea after plea to beekeepers not to undersell their product."

1990 made a good start with an above average year; **Jeff** reported that his foray up to the heather provided his best crop ever. Should we take too much notice of **Jeff** from this point on; he had recently retired, and now only ran some 150 hives! Happily I can vouch for him; I wrote in a **CBKA Newsletter** that although it had been a swarmy year - 50 calls one day - I had a good honey crop. The Editorial for the 1991, Christmas **BBJ** mentioned: "... correspondence and conversation with beekeepers suggests that the honey harvest has varied from county to county, from good to rather poor . . ." The 1992 **CBKA Year Book** Editorial began: "What a year for UK beekeepers it has been! Our natural complacence concerning the prospects of us ever being affected by Varroa has proved to be ill founded ..." but concluded, "... the year has not been all bad: excellent crops of honey have been recorded due to the wet spring and warm summer..." .1993, two snippets from Editorials from the **BBJ** give a peep at the dreary year, first October: "From a topsy turvy sunless summer," and, arriving back from abroad in November: "... we return to a land flowing with water from torrential rain ... a summer that never was to an autumn that never really materialised ..." **Jeff** speaks of a wonderful 1994 Norfolk honey season in the November **BBJ**, and of an apiarist with thirty hives getting his best crop ever; however, the Editorial for December reports areas of the country under water during November, with more rain predicted. The CBKA Chairman said in the magnificent **Yearbook** for 1995: "Many of us have had a bumper harvest due to the magnificent summer after a mild winter." However, in the next **Yearbook** he began: "1996 has been a year that many beekeepers would perhaps prefer to forget. A late start because of cold weather turned into a difficult summer ..." The Editor in the Autumn, **Beekeepers Quarterly (BKQ)**, just gave a terse: "A mixed year for most, as regards honey yields ..."

1997, in the October, Thorne's **Beekeepers News**, 'Beelines' reports: "Most beekeepers seem to be quite happy with their lot, especially those who took advantage of the heather after the torrential rain in June. Not a vintage year but still one to be remembered;" only to write in 1998: "It has been too wet, too cold, too cloudy and too late for every beekeeper on these islands." In the 1998 Summer **BKQ**, the Editorial, under the heading 'FRUSTRATING SEASON', begins: "The prolonged cool and wet summer we have experienced so far, etc." - and ended the autumn edition Editorial, under the heading, 'THE WEATHER FORECAST', with: "The very long weather forecast for the next century has been released .... Scientists expect greater extremes of weather to occur, etc." My friend Bob Lemon, then Chairman of CBKA writes in the 1999 **Yearbook**: "Honey crops this year seemed to have come in two stages, early and late due to the fluctuations of the weather, but in the end most fruitful." He also writes of an earlier highlight: "with the aid of Bill Clark we collected a swarm of bees from Sainsbury's car park during the third week of FEBRUARY, the bees had been hanging there from the previous summer. Is the climate really changing?"

For the new Millennia, there is less than ever about honey or weather in my available literature! Even in my own diaries - when I retired, I gave over my weather station to the new incumbents - who haven't bothered with rainfall totals. At least friend Richard Steel now passes over his **BeeCrafts** making an additional search area.

2000: the **CBKA, Summer Newsletter** Editorial begins: "What am I doing, wearing thick winter clothes and grateful to be indoors on a Sunday morning in July," later adding: "... the swelteringly hot afternoon of 20th of June seems a distant memory..." Well, at least we know there was one hot day and it certainly looks as if John Phipps believed the long range weather forecast he printed in the 1998 **BKQ**, for in his autumn 2000 editorial we read: "By the time this issue leaves the printers, my wife and I will be on our way to Greece. Our house has been sold, my bees disposed of and we will be making our new home in the Peloponnese." In fact weather was still on his mind when he got to Greece, for his Editorial in the May 2001 **BKQ** begins: "THE CHANGING CLIMATE", at least he gives me another clue on the 2000 year: "Undoubtedly, beekeepers in the UK have had a poor time of it over the last year." The dearth of information continues for 2001, Foot and Mouth disease took up most of the headlines - However the CBKA Chairman mentions in the **Yearbook**: "... after the wet autumn and the late cold spring many colonies were lost but those that survived picked up well which brought an abundance of swarms . ." The 'England' correspondent, Dr Nigel Payne, in the 2002 **BKQ** for November gives more information: "This year will go down as one of the worst years in recent memory for beekeeping in Dorset and probably for the whole of the UK, come to that. Almost every month has broken a weather record of some sort - mainly bad," - although he did get a crop of honey from his woodland apiary at the end of July into August. An advert in a **CBKA Newsletter** perhaps tells us that East Anglia was no better: "Cut Comb Cutter unused £12. Uncapping Knife £10." We must hope Nigel Hurst's correspondence for Scotland, in the November **BKQ** included the rest of Britain: "2003 started altogether differently as we had a very good early crop. The summer lime flow was early and short. The heather which we went to for the first time this year was just wonderful." Ivor Davis in his Guest Editorial for September 2004 **BeeCraft** writes: "I have been hearing stories across the country that this spring was one of the best for a long time but the summer has been poor for honey crops." Dr Payne starts his column in the Autumn **BKQ** for 2005: "Annus Horribilus .... Bad weather throughout spring and early summer appeared to be the cause of all sorts of problems here in Dorset." He also mentioned, that despite a spell of hot weather in July, the honey crop was down 50% on normal!

2006: Despite the **BKQ** for September being a special honey issue, neither the bee farmers or Nigel Payne mention yields, nevertheless they both mention a cold late spring and later heat and dryness, although it appeared that showers did catch some flowering crops at the right time. Colin Weightman in **BeeCraft** - after writing that the severe weather over Europe missed the UK at last mentions: "made up colonies subsequently filled several supers each." The 2007 **BeeCraft** has Claire Waring describing the Royal Show as "Wet, Wet, Wet," and a letter from a beekeeper describes how he found his hives under two feet of water. In the October edition, Bob Gilbert says that during a two day beekeeping course: "The weather was kind, the rain stopped each time we went outside!" However, Don Hannon mentioned in the December issue - whilst writing about the "National", that he had an Indian Summer into November. Memories of 2008 are still raw for most of us, but I must still put it into print - no need to search far. First the Editorial in the **CBKA Newsletter**: "Well, how was it for you? What kind of a year have you had? For me, I had a good start to the year and it went down hill from there." And from the Chair: "What a terrible year for beekeeping this has been. After the severe losses over the winter the weather has been so bad that there is now a serious lack of honey," and lastly, the Honey Show Secretary: "I suppose a poor season for many of us was bound to lead to a reduced number of exhibits this year."

And so, here we are at 2009. My own contribution for the Summer **CBKA Newsletter** was that it was my busiest year for swarms since Varroa arrived, and the Winter Editorial commented, "Lets also hope for a better honey crop next year." The **BeeCraft** editorial for December, says it is good to reflect on the past season - but then doesn't! The Bee Farmers in the September **BKQ** speak of a mixed story over the country, whilst Nigel Payne writes: "What an exciting year it has been," before mentioning how well his bees have recovered since the disastrous winter losses, and how the sun shone when he needed it for the oil seed rape. The Bee Farmers relate in the November issue that Scotland's "weather has meant that honey crops have been exceptionally poor," and Nigel Payne reports: ".... some wag in the meteo profession promised us a 'barbecue summer' . . . What happened? The wettest July since 1888!" However, he did end up with a honey harvest. Even The Times waded in - sorry about that - with a four page spread on the 1st of December about the wet weather: "November may have broken national rainfall records ...," some rain facts that included: "2000 tonnes per year for every person in Engand," and also on ways to enjoy it!

Well; this weather report has taken some weeks, and it has been enlightening, to say the least. But I think only in as much as it proves we all have very short memories. If asked, even I may have said: "Ah yes, we had many, really long, beautiful summers during my childhood!" We may now be having milder winters, and earlier springs, but it is obvious that our 'green and pleasant land' is only because of the rainfall. As I type this on the 27th of April 2010, the sun is shining, my bees are working well, but after no measurable rain for over a month, my garden is dry - I think we need a good rain!

FOR THE WORKSHOP

John Phipps

Introduction

This method of making the frame is not the inspired genius of R. Raff who visited me in August, (and watched with obvious embarrassment as I constructed it) but dedicated to him, for his articles suggest to me that the maxim "Better is the enemy of good enough" is one with which he has a great deal of empathy. This method of construction is also dedicated to John Alien who has perfected the art of re-cycling and whose creativity and resourcefulness cannot surely be matched. I am a strong believer in the efficaciousness and simplicity which this method of treatment offers against varroa. Thymol crystals are also relatively cheap when compared with other acaricides and being a natural product and one which beekeepers are already familiar with, I am not surprised that this method seems to be gaining popularity.

One of the problems is, of course, that in order for varroa treatment to work effectively, then all colonies need to be treated simultaneously. At ten pounds a go, the commercially produced Frakno frame may work out quite expensive, especially if tens of colonies are being run. A careful look at a completed frame (or the plans in previous editions of the BKQ) suggest that someone with access to a circular saw will have no difficulty in making up a batch of the frames.

However, there are some fiddily cuts to be made with the saw and unless one has good skills with such a machine they are best left alone (I have seen the ends of Raff's fingers!).

Materials

The Raff/Allen frame can easily be made with the simplest of tools — just an ordinary saw, a hammer and a penknife. All the bits and pieces needed for the frame are likely to be found in any beekeeper's shed: an old brood frame, a piece of thin sheet material or some old section pieces, eight old bottom bars, some frame nails, glue, wire cloth and a piece of scrim-like material.

Method of Construction

1. Obtain an old brood frame suited to the hives that you use. Cut away the top bar BETWEEN the two sides of the frame and nail in place further down the sides of the frame so that it will, if required, allow the fitting of a piece of drone super foundation.

2. Cut two pieces, 1 3/4" wide of thin plywood, hardboard, plastic, (or, as I used,a length of section — the wide parts being trimmed away with a penknife) to the same external dimensions of the frame. Nail or glue in place so that the top of each strip is level with the bottom of the lugs. This will make the sides of the trough to hold the crystals.

3. Cut to length two old bottom bars of a frame and glue and pin to the bottom inside of the trough sides.

4. **Cut** two more **bottom** bar strips and glue and pin beneath strips already fitted to trough sides. Onto these two pieces, cut to size and staple or stick chosen permeable gauze for crystals to vapourise through.

5. Cut to length four more bottom bars and stick two of each together. Use a piece of the trough side material as a spacer, and then pin and glue each piece to the side bars so that a saw width slot is made beneath and also below the centre of the trough.

6. Cut wire cloth to size to fit over the top of the trough.

12 g of thymol crystals are put in the trough and the frame remains in place until all the crystals have evaporated.

NATIONAL HONEY SHOW EXHIBIT, 2009

HONEY SHOWS

R Raff

Brad, a two-year-old whippet bred at Filey, north Yorkshire, was the winner of two best-of-show awards in Britain. After being sold to a new owner in America he was bunged on a plane and six hours later arrived in Philadelphia. When he was being led from the plane he broke free and bunked off. I suppose it was natural for him to do a runner; after all he was a whippet. Sadly, his bid for freedom was short-lived because he ran across a railway and was struck by a train and killed.

I'm sure we as beekeepers can appreciate how the poor owner must have felt. It's not the first time some of us have introduced a queen to a stock only to have the bees kill her. This is bad enough if it is a queen we have bred ourself, but it is worse when we have paid good money for her. It is possible, of course, that some of the other whippet owners breathed a sigh of relief to know that a bit of formidable competition had been eliminated.

Thinking about Brad winning these prizes and "formidable competition" made me think of honey shows. By the time this appears in print they will be in full swing and I started to wonder about them. Why do we have them? What purpose do they serve? Could they be made more attractive? Where does the public figure in them, if at all? Do they help us to sell more honey? Do they spur us on to have top class honey for sale? I recall the first time I ever entered a show. Afterwards, when we were circulating, I asked a man who was a renowned exhibitor how he obtained his prize winning cakes of wax not realising that I was perhaps putting him in a difficult situation. . He started to tell me but only got three or four sentences out when his wife muttered out of the corner of her mouth "Don't tell him how you do it". The Freemasons tell us that they are not a secret society, but do admit to being a society with secrets. In my innocence I figured that this honey show business must be run on similar lines.

Unlike the Freemasons I do not have secrets and I am quite happy to tell how I go about preparing my exhibits for honey shows. I have what I call my "everlasting honey" and this is a great time and labour saving device. I stumbled on it by accident years ago and it has served me well and I could just about paper a room with all my prize winning tickets.

It all started when I selected jars from my ordinary sale stock of honey and heated them up until they were well and truly liquid. I did this in a pan of water with strips of wood under the jars. I skimmed any froth, saw that the jars had no flaws, good lids, clean wads, stood them in the sunlight and bingo, prize winners. They were laid aside and hauled out for the next show and given another good cooking and they brought in more tickets. It got to a stage when they never showed any sign of granulation and their clarity and moisture content was wonderful. It's just as well the judges had no way of testing for HMF. As time went on all I had to do was make sure that the wads were clean. I also had my supply of shallow frames. The capping was perfection although the honey was like concrete and they too made their way to show after show and collared me tickets.

Now, am I being unfair or underhand? The schedules don't say that the honey has to be of the current season and indeed for those shows with a heather class, the honey would usually have to be of the previous year. It's true this honey of mine is so old and been in so many shows it could just about find its own way there, but is it my blame that it keeps winning prizes? Is it the judge's fault, or the fault of other competitors for not producing better exhibits? I have little time for people who say that it is not the winning that counts, but the taking part. That is rubbish. I have a grand-daughter who is now a grown woman. When she was a little girl, four or five years old, I would take her putting. If she was in danger of losing she would pick up the ball and drop it in the hole. When I remonstrated she would say vehemently, "But grand-dad, I've GOT TO WIN!" I'm all for the competitive spirit as long as it does not get out of hand. Another child I know in whom the spirit was strong, was even worse, and she was, indeed, a vicious little hussy.

I have to tell you, I have never mastered the art of producing good wax exhibits so I do not waste my time on them. With judges it is a case of what they prefer. One will think nothing of frosting for instance whereas another won't like it and you are just at their mercy. Kind of like John Denver, the country singer who was killed recently when his plane crashed. For a lark he entered a "JOHN DENVER LOOK ALIKE COMPETITION" and even sang one of his best known songs, "Take me back country roads". He came in third.

UNLIKE SOME PEOPLE, I HAVE NEVER BEEN ABLE TO MASTER THE ART OF PRODUCING GOOD WAX EXHIBITS.

The majority of honey shows in this country are geared solely to beekeepers and I think that is where they fall down. They should be geared to the public with a view to encouraging them to buy British honey and enlightening them on bees and beekeeping. Beekeepers are in a very privileged position. In company, if someone says they are a President of the Golf Club, Secretary of the Cricket Club or Treasurer of the Bowling Club, they don't usually get much of a hearing. Let it be known that you are a beekeeper and immediately you have their attention. You are up there with the sword swallower, tightrope walker, lion tamer, fire eater and so on. Yes, you are someone and the shows should cash in on this.

There could be a whole range of honeys there for people to sample. And people there to answer their questions. Prize winning exhibits could all be put up for sale. Exhibits could be taken for testing for HMF, for example, and if they failed, the awards could be withdrawn. Frames of honey could be made identifiable in case they appeared in other shows. Yes, I think Honey Shows should be subjected to a radical overhaul and a lot could be done to keep people like me out of shows. As I write that it makes me think of Groucho Marx when he said that he would not want to belong to any club that would have HIM for a member. In my case, as things stand and in fairness to myself, the public are protected because I would never sell any of my prize winning exhibits. Well I can't afford to. They're my stock in trade. After all, when Brad the whippet won his first award they didn't take him out and shoot him, did they?

PEOPLE HAVE MORE AFFINITY WITH DOGS THAN HONEY JARS!

For members of the public to wander into a honey show, even the prestigious National Honey Show, must be one of the most deadly boring experiences of their life. If they wandered into a dog show at least they could identify with some of the animals. A Lurcher would immediately make them think of Claude Greengrass and his dog Alfred in "Heartbeat". A Border Terrier would remind them of Butch Dingle's dog in "Emmerdale". A Border Collie, and there they are with Phil Drabble at the sheepdog trials. There's plenty they could identify with but it is hard for them to work up an interest over rows of bottles of honey even though they are different colours. I can only think of one other experience that might be more boring than a honey show and that is a game of Scrabble. At least at a honey show they are on their feet and there is not the same danger of falling asleep.

While members of the public may be in danger of falling asleep this cannot be said of the Honey Judges. They have a very demanding job to do and have to be on their toes and I must congratulate George Hawthorne on completing fifty years of this work. Mention was made in Newsround last issue about his testing rods and grading glasses. These are only two of the items a Honey Judge must have when s/he reports for duty. I would like he or someone else to tell us just exactly what all has to be taken along when judging because the paraphernalia required is unbelievable. It's a list as long as your arm!

From The Beekeepers Quarterly, No 54, Summer 1998

DONALD SIMS

THE BEST BEE IS THE ONE THAT SUITS YOUR LOCALITY

Donald Sims NDB

Among many beekeepers the current fashion is for the re-creation and reinstatement of the old English dark bee. Much of current bee breeding work has that aim. Its advocates consider it to be the best bee for use in Britain, and say so, and seek purity of race through wing venation measurements. A coordinated effort to improve our bees is highly desirable, which I would support if I could, but I am not persuaded that this is the best way forward, or that the old dark bee had such desirable qualities as its advocates allege. The belief is based on myth and not on fact. It is thought to have had superior qualities to most of the bees that we beekeepers currently have. I doubt that. Certainly it had some good qualities, but it also had more bad ones.

Is the native dark bee the best bee for us to use in Britain? Not one of those who wrote about bees in the quarter century following the introduction of the Ligurian bee in 1859 was of that opinion. Woodbury (1863), Neighbour (1866), Hunter (1876), Cheshire (1876), Robinson (1880), and Samson (1882), all considered that bees had been greatly improved by the introduction of the Ligurian blood, and said so. Of the native dark bee the comment that - and I quote - *"it had many inferior qualities, among which we may list excitable under manipulation, great susceptibility to disease, tolerance of wax moth and other qualities associated with a poor house cleaning bee",* fairly summarised their opinions, they considered the Ligurian bee to be - and again I quote - *"superior to the native dark bee in wintering ability, in temper, in industriousness, and as house cleaners."* But these opinions of writers who had first hand experience of the native dark bee and could compare it with an imported race (the Ligurian) receive no mention and are totally ignored. And with varroa here to stay we need a super house cleaning bee, not a poor one.

It is, of course, a common human folly to welcome confirmation of one's preconceived notions while ignoring or rejecting contrary views. But it destroys credibility and leads to ill considered action and subsequent disappointment. It leads to presentation of supportive conclusions as facts when they may not be well founded or may even be known to be based on slight evidence.

When I worked with Barnes, around Lydd and Dungeness, in the twenties, his bees were pretty yellow. "Goldens" he called them, though I have since seen bees that were far more golden than his. He had kept bees a long time, and had lost his colonies from the so called Isle of Wight Disease some years before. But I recall that he had no doubt that his "Goldens" were better than the dark bees he had lost - they got more honey, were easier to handle, steadier on the combs, and worked sections - his speciality - equally well, he said. I recall too that when I first met Brother Adam at Rothampsted in 1935, his opinion, based on his own first hand experience with western European dark bees in earlier years, was much the same. He considered their undesirable traits to outweigh their good qualities.

It may be that current efforts will produce a bee with all the merits and none of the faults of the old English dark bee. I am not too optimistic about that. Nevertheless it makes good sense to take positive steps *"to conserve, select and improve our native and near native strains of honeybees",* which are the stated aims of BIBBA. At least it will preserve valuable genetic material and at best it will provide many beekeepers with bees to their liking. But I don't go along at all with the dismissive attitude that devotees of the old English dark bee breeding programme evidently have to other races and strains of honeybees. Modern bee breeding techniques make it possible to develop strains of bee for a variety of purposes, and we are, in my view, fortunate in the UK in having such a varied gene bank on which to draw.

In Northumberland Ernie Pope and I bred queens that were mated in a remote spot in Kielder Forest. To the best of our knowledge there were no other bees within seven miles. Our breeding effort was based on breeder queens that I had from J.E. Hasting after a visit to him in northern Saskatchewan, with daughter queens from these crossed with dark Northumbrian drones. Hasting said his bees were Caucasian, but Brother Adam said they were largely Carniolan, and I notice that Hasting's sons now offer Carniolan queens for sale, not Caucasian. Be that as it may, the resultant queens and their colonies were very much to our liking, and they did very well in Northumberland, both on the heather and on earlier flows. We had twelve years experience with them. But they were not the best bees for Cambridgeshire and Essex, with the early flows from the rape and nothing much after mid July.

MID NINETEENTH CENTURY IMPORTERS OF LIGURIAN BEES FOUND THAT THEIR 'GOLDENS' HAD SOME CHARACTERISTICS WHICH WERE BETTER THAN NATIVE BEES.

My breeding programme has always been based on performance, and I think I have bees well suited to their location and to my system of management. But they are not the same bees that I had in Northumberland, or, for that matter, that I had in Devon or Kent. You still need a bee well suited to your district if you look for good performance.

From Sixty Years with Bees,
The Beekeepers Quarterly, No 37, Spring 1994.

A BEE HOUSE FOR BEE BREEDING

John Atkinson NDB

Bee breeding in the British Isles is difficult enough without putting obstacles in the way. One of the bigger obstacles is the weather. Putting breeding stock and rearing colonies out in the open air exposes the colonies to the weather.

Bee Breeding at its most basic is the rearing of drones from a particular queen, and the rearing of the virgin queens that the drones are to be used on, and timing these two operations so that enough drones will be sexually mature six days after the virgins have hatched. It means working to a timetable, quite a precise timetable. A force nine gale, a cold spell, heavy rain; all can play havoc with that timetable.

Putting up with avoidable havoc is just not on. Well, not with me. It can be avoided by having the drone rearing and the queen rearing stocks indoors, and that is where mine are.

It so happened that there is a big loft over part of a range of outbuildings at my home. Before my time, windows had been put in the walls of this loft. I decided to convert this loft to a bee house. The decision was not as obvious as it sounds. The building is of stone and the walls are eighteen inches thick. I started with an end wall, the south wall, chiselling out stones until I had made a hole right the way through. 1 did not make all six holes at once as that would have risked the wall collapsing. I put in 2" grey plastic pipe, making a hole in the brood chamber where the pipe came through on the inside. I went to a lot of trouble to make good the wall, so that it not only looked all right, but to make sure it was really strong.

It did not work. Few bees ever found the way out. Working from the outside I had to set to and cut out all my carefully done stonework for a depth of a foot. I remade the entrances for each of the six hives with an agricultural drainage "tile", that is the foot long unglazed pottery pipe traditionally used for land drainage. These pipes 1 painted on the inside with an exterior grade white paint, made for stonework, one of the plastic based paints. I retained the original grey plastic pipe for the inner six inches of the wall. The hole in the brood chamber was covered over. An eke (actually a "nadir") was made, through the end of which the pipe passed. This system worked and I used it throughout; for the six hives along the south wall, and subsequently for the eight along the west wall.

What is a bit of a nuisance is the "summer only" nature of my bee house. I am not sure why I cannot winter bees in it. It may be that my alteratons to the entrance pipes were not sufficiently drastic. It may be the exposure, the lack of shelter at first floor level. It may be something else. After a number of trials that all failed, I now move the colonies out to wintering sites at the end of the season.

In most bee houses I have seen, the stocks are too low; they are too close to the floor. Mine are supported eighteen inches above floor level on benching made from second hand 3" by 2" studding. I have found this gives firm support and an excellent working height. Proper working height is important, particularly if you suffer from beekeeper's back. I may say I have never understood the rationale of having two layers of hives in a bee house. If one layer is at the best working height, the other cannot be. If you need to gel more hives in, face the fact that you need a larger bee house, or a second one.

For ease of working I have a gap between each hive. Six inches or so, measured from side wall to side wall, seems to work all right.

Mention of side walls brings up the question of what brood chamber to use. This, in a bee house for bee breeding, should be determined, first by the frame you use, and then by your height. I use BS frames. I use them because they are the standard. If you are a Langstroth devotee, use Langstroth. The frame pattern makes little difference for bee breeding work, provided "over square" patterns are avoided. By over square I mean patterns in which the depth of the frame is greater than the width, as in one of the Continental patterns.

Now your height. My height - in shoes - is five foot nine-ish. I therefore use a sixteen frame brood chamber.

Bees in a bee house must have their combs "warm way", that is parallel to the hive front. I can comfortably reach across to the sixteenth frame but no further. Somebody over six foot perhaps could manage seventeen frames. For a short person sixteen frames are probably too many.

For some purposes, cell builder stocks for instance, exceedingly strong colonies are required. It is a great advantage in a bee house, if such strong colonies can, none the less, be limited to two storeys of deep combs. It is a fairly simple matter to plan somewhere in the bee house for putting down an upper brood chamber full of bees. It is quite another matter to have to find space for two, both boiling over with bees, while you are going through the third and bottom brood chamber. I find a sixteen frame lower chamber with an eleven frame standard upper chamber enables me to have stocks marginally stronger than that recommended for American commercial queen rearing. I use mounted National queen excluders. The upper chamber goes over the twelve frames nearest the wall of the bee house. I use a home made crownboard for the four frames left uncovered in the lower chamber. This arrangement has the great advantage that a certain amount of necessary swapping of combs between the two chambers can be done without taking the upper chamber off.

My one builder colony is arranged this way, as is my starter support colony, the colony that provides young bees for stocking the swarm box. I find a single sixteen frame box of deep combs is fine for a virgin nursery. The breeder queens, in their half frame inserts, are each in a single National shallow box. The drone mothers are on single frame shallow boxes, sometimes with a National shallow super, which is used for breeder support.

Windows.

For years bee losses against window panes and windows were a problem. The books suggest that as bees move up, you should arrange for weather protected escape at the top. I did. It would not be fair to say it does not work, as some bees do manage to escape that way, but many get tired before they get to the top of the window. On windows with panes, losses are particularly bad, each glazing bar being a barrier.

Finally I had a window made to my own design to try. I tried it for a season. It worked a treat. 1 have now replaced a second window, and would have replaced the lot by now, but for the cost. The window, which can be opened, consists of a single piece of glass. Indeed part of the strength of the window is in the glass itself. For this reason I use 5 mm glass. It is expensive - but not nearly as expensive as the 6 mm stuff stocked locally. The glass goes into grooves made down the centre of the two hefty side members. Metal plates are let into the bottom of the side members to stop the glass sliding out. Two cross members, one at the top and one at the bottom are fixed across the inner face of the side members, the face facing into the loft. This allows about a half inch gap between these members and the glass. Each window is swivel hinged.

For the bee loft itself the windows are constructed so that there is a gap top and bottom with the window fully closed. For the grafting room window it will be necessary to open the window slightly for a gap. The grafting room, which occupies a corner of the loft, houses the with-bees cell incubator, and is the room used for loading queens into travelling cages. Thus on some occasions the room must be bee tight, and on others it is necessary to get rid of flying bees.

Feeding.

It is a cardinal principle of queen rearing that there should be a moderate flow, and that in the absence of one, feeding should be continuous. What it boils down to is that feeding should be continuous, for should one be lucky enough to have a flow the bees will ignore the feeder. The filled feeder will, however, be ready and waiting for the moment when the flow stops. Few beekeepers appreciate that this business of continuous feeding applies with even greater importance to drone rearing and maturing.

It seemed to me sensible to take this recommendation of continuous feeding literally every hive. This obviates the risk of a conventional feeder running dry, saves most of the work of feeder filling, and removes one of the risks attendant on drone production. There are problems, of course, with continuous syrup feeding. One of these is fermentation. My experience is that if syrup for queen rearing stocks is made as weak as the Americans (Contemporary Queen Rearing) suggest, then there are fermentation problems in a piped system; fermentation problems that thymol, at several times the recommended dose, will not prevent.

Full strength syrup (8 kg to 5 1, or 2 lb to a pint) overcomes the problem - but in an unacceptable way, for the bees take the stuff down too fast. The aim is to simulate a moderate flow. A heavy flow is harmful. Apart from this, the cost rules out this approach.

There are problems in bee house beekeeping. One of these in my bee loft is the light level. I suspect this may apply to bee houses generally. Combs that need close examination I generally take outside the door. I go to one of the windows only when compelled by bad weather.

The problem of light is particularly acute with the half frame inserts. If the insert is left in the hive while the combs in the queen's compartment are examined, the queen escapes while you have gone to look at a comb. I tried to get over this by taking the entire insert to a table by one of the windows. This worked for much of the time, but was none the less a disaster, as a season did not go by without the loss of one, sometimes more than one breeder queen. I did not find the queens dead. They disappeared. It was a long time before I found the cause. The insert is, in effect, a tiny hive. Once the top is off, the queen has not got to move far to be out and away. If you do not realise this has happened and if the insert is away from the hive, you lose the queen.

JOHN ATKINSON 'S BEE HOUSE FOR BEE BREEDING

When I realised what was happening I was able to put it right with what I call my Samaritans' Board. With the insert on the table by the window the board, guided by its runners, is slid over the open portion until it reaches the glass covering the queen's compartment. It then pushes the glass before it until the opening in the board fully exposes the queen's compartment. A queen intent on escaping now has to traverse the wide board where she is easily seen and her escape attempts thwarted. The Samaritans' Board has put a stop to royal suicides.

My bee loft is a godsend from May to August. Perhaps one day I will have a purpose made bee house as well for early drone production.

Finally, I must stress that I am writing about the bee house solely in relation to bee breeding. George Hawthorne in the January '89 Beekeepers News puts bee houses for honey production in perspective. For that purpose he does not like them - and neither would I.

JOHN GLEED COLLECTING RUSHES FOR SKEP MAKING.

MAKE YOUR OWN SKEP AND REVIVE AN OLD CRAFT

JOHN GLEED, SCOTLAND

Most skep beekeepers would, of course, construct their own hives from materials which were found abundantly in their locality, but more importantly, materials which were free. Today, the traditional waste products from arable farming are straw and baler twine, though each of these can present problems. Modern cereals are bred to be shorter, or are treated with growth regulators, to prevent the crop from lodging - that is falling over in wet weather - particularly towards harvest time. Rye straw, if available, makes good skeps and is still usually very long. Baler twine can disintegrate over the years if the skep is exposed to the sun and if the plastic hasn't been treated with an ultra-violet light inhibitor. Rushes have the advantage of being over four feet long. If available they should be collected in autumn and hung up to dry.

1. Materials. Straw or reeds, scissors, baler twine, preferably the thick twine from small square bales, chipboard disc 7" in diameter and 3/4" or 1" thick with thirty-six holes drilled approximately' 1/4" from edge, sack needle or needle for trussing fowls and a filler approximately 2" wide at one end and 1 1/2" at the other.

2. & 3. To start, heat end of string and form a point. Thread through hole and tie eight or ten straws which have been laid on the disc thin ends first.

4. Proceed by inserting more straws thick ends first from now on. The needle will not be needed till all thirty-six holes have been used.

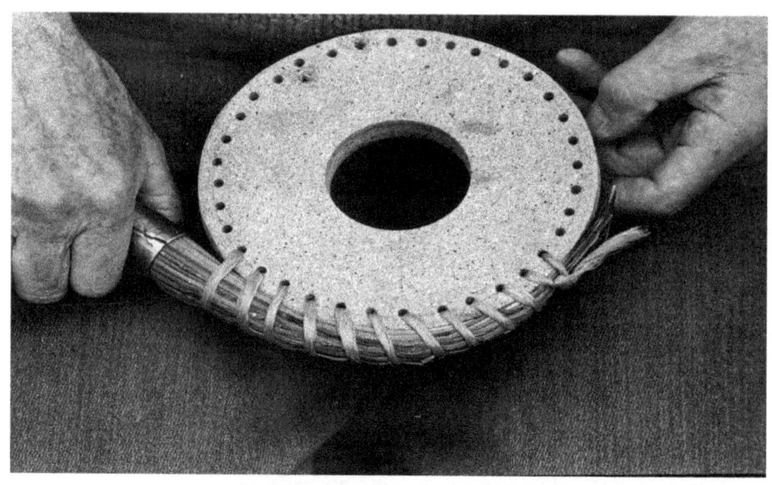

5. & 6. By the time ten or twelve holes have been used the rope will be thick enough for the filler to be put on. Straws should be added continually, rammed into the centre of the rope under the forefinger and the filler kept packed. It should be so tight that it can hardly be moved. This is especially important at the end of a session.

7. & 8. When more string is needed leave tails about 2" long and hide tails and knot between the coils. When the last hole has been filled the needle will now be used and stitching begins. This is the time to decide whether to make the skep flat-topped or domed. This is determined by the angle of the stitching.

9. Continue working the coils until you have the skep the required size.

10. Making the door. A matter of choice whether to have the door in the skep or in the floor. If only for taking swarms no door is needed.

11. To finish the skep stop inserting straw and let the rope taper off.

From The Beekeepers Quarterly No 41, Spring 1995.

STEVE TABER

DRONES AS INDICATORS OF A COLONY'S CONDITION

STEVE TABER

The vast majority of beekeepers don't like drones and rip out the drone brood when they find it in their hives. But the drones, the presence or absence of them, are an indicator and what they indicate or tell you about the hive's condition is what this article is about. The presence or absence of drone brood in the hive is used as an indicator of food sufficiency. Of course, there are exceptions to this generalization, so first we will talk about the exceptions.

The most important exception occurs in late summer or early fall in the north, when the first cold snap comes along with a killing frost. At that time of year there are plenty of stores in the hive so bees are not starving. But something tells the bees at that time, and I have no idea what it is, they no longer need drones. The adults are expelled from the hives and the drone eggs, larvae and pupae are eaten. Some books tell of this event as the "slaughter of the drones". In the southern part of the country (USA), where I live, we do not get this drastic event. At least, I have never seen it because the bees don't have any drones to speak of at that time of year in their hives, anyway.

But in states like Wisconsin and New York, where I have worked, it is really dramatic. One day in January while I was a student at the University of Wisconsin, I was having an argument with Dr Farrar about this - the fact that bees killed off all

DRONES ARE GOOD INDICATOR'S OF A COLONY'S CONDITION.

drones in their hives in the fall. Farrar said, "No, some remain". We kept arguing and he had other work to do, so he flipped me the keys of the truck and told me to go look for myself.

There was snow on the ground and the temperature was about 15 degrees F and the wind was blowing. I will never know how an 'ol Southern boy like me was able to survive four winters in Wisconsin. Man, it gets cold there! So here I was driving out to a bee yard all prepared to pry open a colony of bees just to prove it did not have drones.

At that time Farrar wintered all his colonies 3 high in full depth Langstroth boxes with the top box packed solid with honey. There were no bees in the top box. After a struggle I was able to get it loose from its frozen position and lifted it off where I encountered the bees.

When it is this cold the bees cannot move; all they do is stick their rear ends up at you, pointing their stingers right smack at the closest part of you. Some of you should try opening a hive on a really cold winter day. Try to pry the centre comb out and up, with that cluster of bees all stuck together like glue. It is a very difficult task with 10 frames or combs in a 10 frame box. Farrar always kept 9 in each box - as I do. This way, when a comb is removed, you don't roll the bees. It tends to get them very angry.

The centre comb and the centre of the cluster was comb 5 - and I succeeded with a great effort in getting it loose and pulling it free. The bees inside the cluster are warm and, as soon as the comb is pulled up about 2 or 3 inches, those warm bees fly straight at you backward with their stings stuck straight out. Bee men are born to suffer; otherwise why be a beekeeper?

And yes, there were drones. 30 or 40 of them. And a small patch of worker brood too. That was a problem I always had with Farrar. He always knew exactly what was in every bee hive all the time. And, I will tell you, that is exasperating. He had always said "Queens will begin to lay eggs about the first of the year and will continue if they don't run out of pollen". Why, why, why would bees start rearing brood this far from spring and with no blooming flowers to provide them with food? Where I have worked in southern parts of the US there is almost always something blooming all winter. On warm days, that is, warm enough for bees to fly, you will see them bringing in pollen. You should expect to see brood, that is small amounts, at all times of the year. But in Wisconsin? No way! ... But there it was!

The other exception to bees rearing drones is when the colony has a failing queen or has been queenless for a time and some of the worker bees are laying eggs. By the time you have kept 4 or 5 colonies for 10 years or so you will most likely have seen both of these rather peculiar events.

But let's get back to the main theme of using drones as an indicator. What does the presence of drones, adult and immature tell you? Remember how the bees are behaving and what they are doing in the mid-spring period until the mid summer period? During that part of the bee season when you open a hive and look in the brood nest you usually see every drone cell occupied with an immature drone, a pupa or larva. Because most beekeepers remove combs containing drone comb, the bees in their desperation build comb between brood chambers and fill it with drone brood.

If you have a number of colonies, say 20 or more, and have kept bees for 5 or 6 years, you most likely have experienced a period of time in the late spring when all of the bees look like a million. You think you are going to have the best season ever. But then you get hit by a cold, rainy period that seems to never end. You know the bees don't have much stores to tide them over and you don't want to feed sugar because as soon as the sun comes out your bees will be in a major honey flow. Finally, you look, and you see the worst thing that can happen, all your bees are starving. But now look a bit longer, you will see no drones, either adult or mature. The bees have eaten or killed them.

Years ago, when I was reading about bees - trying to learn something, the author commented that the reason the bees raised so many drones was to use them as surplus food. So if you really notice what is going on in your hive with the drone brood, the young drone brood will sometimes disappear over night. Think about that for a moment - a fully developed drone larva has almost enough nutrition to feed two worker larvae! Drone pupae, the bees can't eat these very well, so they throw them out the entrance; and some of you have seen that.

THE INEDIBLE DRONE PUPAE ARE REMOVED FROM THEIR CELLS AND THROWN OUT OF THE ENTRANCE.

The spring buildup period is very **critical** for your bees; and if you are expecting and hoping to have your bees make a big crop of honey, you can't get that by subjecting them to starvation 15 minutes before the honey flow starts.

As a postscript; another very important indicator drones are good for is to capture the varroa mite. There are two parts to this, the first is as biological varroa control. This technique was developed by some European scientists years ago and simply involves placing full sheets of drone brood in the centre of the brood nest. When the drone brood has pupated, the comb is removed and discarded and another one placed from where it was removed. This technique is successful because the mites prefer and actively seek out drone brood to reproduce on. No chemicals are used and the mite populations are reduced.

The second part is to use drone pupae to determine the mite infestation rate. The drone pupae are uncapped and removed from their cells and the percent of infested larvae are determined. If you count 50% or more pupae infested, the colony should be treated with Apistan or Bayvarol strips. However, if a honey flow is in progress, wait to treat until you have removed your honey crop.

From The Beekeepers Quarterly No 57, Spring 1999.

I thank Thee, God, that I have lived
In this great world and known its many joys;
The song of birds, the strong sweet scent of hay
And cooling breezes in the secret dusk,
The flaming sunsets at the close of day,
Hills, and the lonely, heather-covered moors,
Music at night, and moonlight on the sea,
The beat of waves upon the rocky shore
And wild, white spray, flung high in ecstasy;
The faithful eyes of dogs, and treasured books,
The love of kin and fellowship of friends,
And all that makes life dear and beautiful.
I thank Thee, too, that there has come to me
A little sorrow and, sometimes, defeat,
A little heartache and the loneliness
that comes with parting, and the word, "Goodbye",
dawn breaking after dreary hours of pain,
when I discovered that night's gloom must yield
and morning light break through to me again.
Because of these and other blessings poured
Unasked upon my wondering head,
Because I know that there is yet to come
An even richer and more glorious life,
And most of all, because Thine only Son
Once sacrificed life's loveliness for me -
I thank Thee, God, that I have lived!

A Poem in Appreciation of Life and the Wonders of Nature
(sent to the editor by Joanne Mobus shortly after the death of her husband).

The poem was written by Elizabeth Craven, writer and socialite (1750 - 1828).

11 DIARY & CALENDAR

- PART II -

***SR (SUNRISE) SS (SUNSET) FOR LONDON UK.**

Notes and photographs by the Editor.

JANUARY

England used to be called the "Isle of Honey" or
"Yr Fel Ynys" which meant the "Land of Milk and Honey"

Every drop of nectar which the bees collect to turn into honey is of immense value. With careful management the beekeeper can ensure that the working life of the foraging bee is not wasted. Bees are living in an increasingly alien environment and only with the beekeepers help are they now able to survive as strong, functioning colonies. Beekeepers, therefore, have an enormous responsibility for the welfare of their bees.

DAY	JANUARY 2011 FORAGE	TEMP MIN	TEMP MAX	WIND DIR	WIND B.S	CL'D	RAIN	HIVE WEIGHT 1	HIVE WEIGHT 2	HIVE WEIGHT 3
1										
2										
3										
4										
5										
6										
7										
8										
9										
10										
11										
12										
13										
14										
15										
16										
17										
18										
19										
20										
21										
22										
23										
24										
25										
26										
27										
28										
29										
30										
31										

JAN11

	8,SA SR 08:04, SS 16:10
1,SA NEW YEAR'S DAY SR 08:06, SS 16:01	9,SU
2,SU	**10,MO**
3,MO	**11,TU**
4,TU ●	**12,WE**
5,WE	**13,TH**
6,TH	**14,FR**
7,FR	15,SA SR 07:59, SS 16:20

16,SU	**24,MO**
17,MO	**25,TU**
18,TU	**26,WE**
19,WE ○	**27,TH**
20,TH	**28,FR**
21,FR	29,SA SR 07:33, SS 16:56
22,SA SR 07:52, SS 16:31	30,SU
23,SU	**31,MO**

FEBRUARY

St Valentine has always been associated with bees as they are a symbol of love. In both European and Asian folk lore, the bee helps a young man to find the right bride.

Recent research in America has shown that over a hundred different pesticides have been found within a hive. Many of these poisonous substances have been absorbed into the wax combs where bees both raise their young and store their food. Regular removal of old combs will help prevent the build up of toxins within the hive, but if pesticide-ridden wax is sent to the manufacturers and recycled as foundation for beekeepers, then the problem is compounded. Many beekeepers are now turning to more sustainable methods of beekeeping which allow the bees to build new combs on to top bars and negates the use of bought-in foundation. Published this year is David Heaf's 'The Bee-friendly Beekeeper' which shows beekeepers how they can change their colony management so that the bees can live more natural, healthy and productive lives.

DAY	FEBRUARY 2011 FORAGE	TEMP MIN	 MAX	WIND DIR	 B.S	CL'D	RAIN	1 HIVE WEIGHT	2	3
1										
2										
3										
4										
5										
6										
7										
8										
9										
10										
11										
12										
13										
14										
15										
16										
17										
18										
19										
20										
21										
22										
23										
24										
25										
26										
27										
28										

FEB11

1,TU

2,WE

3,TH ●

4,FR

5,SA
SR 07:33, SS 16:56

6,SU

7,MO

8,TU

9,WE

10,TH

11,FR

12,SA
SR 07:20, SS 17:09

13,SU

14,MO
ST VALENTINE'S DAY

15,TU

16,WE	**24,TH**
17,TH	**25,FR**
18,FR ○	26,SA SR 06:52, SS 17:34
19,SA SR 07:07, SS 17:22	27,SU
20,SU	**28,MO**
21,MO	
22,TU	
23,WE	

MARCH

In a queenless hive no life is left though to a superficial glance it seems as much alive as other hives.

Full frames of honey stored in fresh new combs will give the honey its best possible light, clear appearance. No chemicals have been used here to drive the bees down from the supers, nor strong jets of air from a bee blower. On a warm still day, when there is still a flow, the honey can be harvested by gently brushing away the bees from the face of the combs - but remembering to leave some food behind for the bees for their immediate needs.

DAY	MARCH 2011 FORAGE	TEMP		WIND		CL'D	RAIN	1	2	3
		MIN	MAX	DIR	B.S			HIVE WEIGHT		
1										
2										
3										
4										
5										
6										
7										
8										
9										
10										
11										
12										
13										
14										
15										
16										
17										
18										
19										
20										
21										
22										
23										
24										
25										
26										
27										
28										
29										
30										
31										

MAR11

	8,TU
1,TU	9,WE
2,WE	10,TH
3,TH	11,FR
4,FR ●	12,SA SR 06:22, SS 17:59
5,SA SR 06:37, SS 17:47	13,SU
6,SU	14,MO
7,MO	15,TU

16,WE

17,TH

18,FR

19,SA ○
SR 06:06, SS 18:11

20,SU
SPRING EQUINOX

21,MO

22,TU

23,WE

24,TH

25,FR

26,SA
SR 05:50, SS 18:23

27,SU
CLOCKS GO FORWARD ONE HOUR

28,MO

29, TU

30, WE

31, TH

APRIL

"Greet the bees on St Zosima's Day and there will be hives and wax."

Uncapping the combs should be done in a warm, clean environment. Here the wax cappings are being removed with an uncapping fork. Some of the best breeds of bees, including *Apis mellifera mellifera*, leave an air space between the honey and the capping. This not only helps the beekeeper to remove the wax more easily, the space helps to prevent honey leaking from combs in the hive during winter, which could lead to fermentation.

DAY	APRIL 2011 FORAGE	TEMP		WIND		CL'D	RAIN	1	2	3
		MIN	MAX	DIR	B.S			HIVE WEIGHT		
1										
2										
3										
4										
5										
6										
7										
8										
9										
10										
11										
12										
13										
14										
15										
16										
17										
18										
19										
20										
21										
22										
23										
24										
25										
26										
27										
28										
29										
30										

APR11

	8,FR
1,FR	9,SA SR 06:19, SS 19:46
2,SA SR 06:34, SS 19:34	10,SU
3,SU ●	11,MO
4,MO	12,TU
5,TU	13,WE
6,WE	14,TH
7,TH	15,FR

16,SA
SR 06:03, SS 19:58

17,SU

18,MO ○

19,TU

20,WE

21,TH

22,FR
GOOD FRIDAY

23,SA
SR 05:49, SS 20:09

24,SU *

25,MO
EASTER MONDAY

26,TU

27,WE

28,TH

29,FR

30,SA
SR 05:35, SS 20:21
ST ZOSIMA AND ST SAVVATIY -
UKRAINIAN PATRON SAINTS OF BEEKEEPING

* ORTHODOX EASTER

MAY

When a bee flies in to your house, expect a visit from a stranger.

Once uncapped, the honey is ready for extraction. Initially, the honey is strained through muslin, over a food quality plastic container, held in place with clothes pegs. Sheets of newspaper cover the floor of the honey house and after any spillage more layers of paper can be added. Trying to wipe floors with water only spreads the honey. After extraction, all the newspaper should be burnt so as not to attract robbing bees. Encourage children to take part in the extraction process, though a finger or two of honey may disappear from the total of honey extracted!

DAY	MAY 2011 FORAGE	TEMP MIN	TEMP MAX	WIND DIR	WIND B.S	CL'D	RAIN	1	2	3
								HIVE WEIGHT		
1										
2										
3										
4										
5										
6										
7										
8										
9										
10										
11										
12										
13										
14										
15										
16										
17										
18										
19										
20										
21										
22										
23										
24										
25										
26										
27										
28										
29										
30										
31										

MAY11

1,SU

2,MO
EARLY MAY BANK HOLIDAY

3,TU ●

4,WE

5,TH

6,FR

7,SA
SR 05:22, SS 20:32

8,SU

9,MO

10,TU

11,WE

12,TH

13,FR

14,SA
SR 05:11, SS 20:43

15,SU

16,MO	24,TU
17,TU ○	25,WE
18,WE	26,TH
19,TH	27,FR
20,FR	28,SA SR 04:53, SS 21:03
21,SA SR 05:01, SS 20:53	29,SU
22,SU	30,MO SPRING BANK HOLIDAY
23,MO	31,TU

JUNE

"The idle drone that labours not at all Sucks up the sweet of honey from the bee."
Shakespeare.

Once strained, the honey has to be stored ready for sale. There are so many types of packaging available today, that the choice is often bewildering. Plastic tubs, glass jars (round, square and hexagonal) as well as tins and bear-shaped squeezy dispensers will add variety to a honey stall. Honey with a good colour will certainly look good in a glass container, whilst for creamed honey a plastic tub for use on the breakfast table would make a suitable choice. As the price of honey has now become generally high, a range of different sizes of containers will provide customers with a product that will suit their pocket.

DAY	JUNE 2011 FORAGE	TEMP		WIND		CL'D	RAIN	1	2	3
		MIN	MAX	DIR	B.S			HIVE WEIGHT		
1										
2										
3										
4										
5										
6										
7										
8										
9										
10										
11										
12										
13										
14										
15										
16										
17										
18										
19										
20										
21										
22										
23										
24										
25										
26										
27										
28										
29										
30										

JUN11

1,WE ●

2,TH

3,FR

4,SA
SR 04:47, SS 21:10

5,SU

6,MO

7,TU

8,WE

9,TH

10,FR

11,SA
SR 04:43, SS 21:16

12,SU

13,MO

14,TU

15,WE ○

16,TH	**24,FR**
17,FR	25,SA SR 04:44, SS 21:21
18,SA SR 04:42, SS 21:20	26,SU
19,SU	**27,MO**
20,MO	**28,TU**
21,TU SUMMER SOLSTICE	**29,WE**
22,WE	**30,TH**
23,TH	

JULY

"When I hear a man preach, I like to see him act as if he were fighting bees."
Abraham Lincoln

Hopefully, beekeepers are no longer as prejudiced as they used to be when labels such as 'British Honey is the Best' used to be used by all and sundry. Many of us are well travelled now and have learnt to respect and love the honeys produced by beekeepers from all parts of the world. The fact that so many varieties of honey are available today - especially in health food shops - shows that customers are more cosmopolitan in their taste and that as beekeepers we must try hard to ensure that our product is of the highest quality, including its presentation.

	JULY 2011	TEMP		WIND		CL'D	RAIN	1	2	3
DAY	FORAGE	MIN	MAX	DIR	B.S			HIVE WEIGHT		
1										
2										
3										
4										
5										
6										
7										
8										
9										
10										
11										
12										
13										
14										
15										
16										
17										
18										
19										
20										
21										
22										
23										
24										
25										
26										
27										
28										
29										
30										
31										

JUL11

	8,FR
1,FR ●	9,SA SR 04:54, SS 21:16
2,SA SR 04:48, SS 21:20	10,SU
3,SU	11,MO
4,MO	12,TU
5,TU	13,WE
6,WE	14,TH
7,TH	15,FR ○

16,SA
SR 05:01, SS 21:10

17,SU

18,MO

19,TU

20,WE

21,TH

22,FR

23,SA
SR 05:10, SS 21:02

24,SU

25,MO

26,TU

27,WE

28,TH

29,FR

30,SA ●
SR 05:20, SS 20:52

31,SU

AUGUST

Like St Ambrose, St Bernard was described as being "honey-tongued" due to his eloquent writings on the love of God. He looked upon bees as symbols of the Holy Ghost.

Many beekeepers use Farmer's Markets or Agricultural Shows as a means of selling their honey. Giving information about each type of honey and allowing the prospective customer to taste samples may well mean the difference between making or losing a sale.

DAY	AUGUST 2011 FORAGE	TEMP		WIND		CL'D	RAIN	1	2	3
		MIN	MAX	DIR	B.S			HIVE WEIGHT		
1										
2										
3										
4										
5										
6										
7										
8										
9										
10										
11										
12										
13										
14										
15										
16										
17										
18										
19										
20										
21										
22										
23										
24										
25										
26										
27										
28										
29										
30										
31										

AUG11

	8,MO
1,MO	9,TU
2,TU	10,WE
3,WE	11,TH
4,TH	12,FR
5,FR	13,SA ○ SR 05:42, SS 20:27
6,SA SR 05:31, SS 20:40	14,SU
7,SU	15,MO

16,TU	**24,WE** ST BARTHOLOMEW'S DAY - TRADITIONAL DAY FOR HARVESTING HONEY
17,WE	**25,TH**
18,TH	**26,FR**
19,FR	27,SA SR 06:04, SS 19:58
20,SA SR 05:53, SS 20:13	28,SU
21,SU ST BERNARD OF CLAIRVAUX	**29,MO** ● SUMMER BANK HOLIDAY
22,MO	**30,TU**
23,TU	**31,WE**

SEPTEMBER

"Books are the bees which carry the quickening pollen from one to another mind."
James Russell Lowell

At some of the larger shows often more than one beekeeper can be present, so the competition for sales increases. Here a beekeeper has brought comb for the customers to try as well as bees in a securely built observation hive. Here the young lad is more interested in the bees than are his mother and sister, who are both intent on trying the comb honey.

DAY	SEPTEMBER 2011 FORAGE	TEMP		WIND		CL'D	RAIN	HIVE WEIGHT		
		MIN	MAX	DIR	B.S			1	2	3
1										
2										
3										
4										
5										
6										
7										
8										
9										
10										
11										
12										
13										
14										
15										
16										
17										
18										
19										
20										
21										
22										
23										
24										
25										
26										
27										
28										
29										
30										

SEP11

	8,TH
1,TH	9,FR
2,FR	10,SA SR 06:26, SS 19:27
3,SA SR 06:15, SS 19:43	11,SU
4,SU	12,MO ●
5,MO	13,TU
6,TU	14,WE
7,WE	15,TH

16,FR	24,SA SR 06:49, SS 18:55
17,SA SR 06:37, SS 19:11	25,SU
18,SU	**26,MO**
19,MO	**27,TU** ●
20,TU	**28,WE**
21,WE	**29,TH**
22,TH	**30,FR**
23,FR AUTUMN EQUINOX	APIMONDIA 42ND INTERNATIONAL APICULTURAL CONGRESS 21-25 SEPTEMBER, BUENOS AIRES

OCTOBER

In the month of Tzec, starting on the 4th October, the Mayans made offerings to their four rain gods. On four separate plates, each of which was bordered with emblems to represent honey, beeswax candles were placed. This custom was to ensure a plentiful supply of flowers and the the people celebrated with honeyed drinks.

Sadly, whilst a shopkeeper might get as much as 30% for selling a beekeeper's honey, often the product is dumped on a shelf and given very little care so that after a while the jars attract dust and the glass loses its sheen. Beekeepers should attempt to be autonomous about the marketing of their honey and here, the beekeeper has not only made her own stand, she also checks the shelves regularly and tops up the spaces and sends in an invoice every month. Additionally, news and photographs can be used to attract and inform customers if space is available. Realistically, any shopkeeper should be pleased with this input from beekeepers as they can gain enormously through extra sales.

DAY	OCTOBER 2011 FORAGE	TEMP		WIND		CL'D	RAIN	1	2	3
		MIN	MAX	DIR	B.S			HIVE WEIGHT		
1										
2										
3										
4										
5										
6										
7										
8										
9										
10										
11										
12										
13										
14										
15										
16										
17										
18										
19										
20										
21										
22										
23										
24										
25										
26										
27										
28										
29										
30										
31										

OCT11

1,SA
SR 07:00, SS 18:39

2,SU

3,MO

4,TU

5,WE

6,TH

7,FR

8,SA
SR 07:11, SS 18:23

9,SU

10,MO

11,TU

12,WE ○

13,TH

14,FR

15,SA
SR 07:23, SS 18:08

16,SU	24,MO
17,MO	25,TU
18,TU	26,WE ●
19,WE	27,TH NATIONAL HONEY SHOW
20,TH	28,FR NATIONAL HONEY SHOW
21,FR	29,SA SR 07:47, SS 17:39 NATIONAL HONEY SHOW
22,SA SR 07:35, SS 17:53	30,SU CLOCKS GO BACK ONE HOUR
23,SU	31,MO

NOVEMBER

"Like bees, they must put their lives into the sting they give."
Ralph Waldo Emerson

How much do you know about honey. Can you easily recognise a honey from its taste, colour and aroma? Could you describe to someone what a particular honey tastes like? Unlike wine, honey has not yet acquired much in the way of a special language to define its sensory nature. However, this could be a good subject for a winter's beekeeping meeting. Honeys, including those from abroad, could be numbered, with participants writing notes on the aroma, taste, texture and colour of the honey, plus an attempt to name the particular variety. After sampling, an interesting discussion should follow - before the honey type is revealed.

DAY	NOVEMBER 2011 FORAGE	TEMP MIN	TEMP MAX	WIND DIR	WIND B.S	CL'D	RAIN	HIVE WEIGHT 1	HIVE WEIGHT 2	HIVE WEIGHT 3
1										
2										
3										
4										
5										
6										
7										
8										
9										
10										
11										
12										
13										
14										
15										
16										
17										
18										
19										
20										
21										
22										
23										
24										
25										
26										
27										
28										
29										
30										

NOV11

	8,TU
1,TU	9,WE
2,WE	10,TH ○
3,TH	11,FR
4,FR	12,SA SR 07:12, SS 16:16
5,SA SR 07:00, SS 16:27	13,SU
6,SU	14,MO
7,MO	15,TU

16,WE	**24,TH**
17,TH	**25,FR** ●
18,FR	26,SA SR 07:35, SS 15:59
19,SA SR 07:24, SS 16:06	27,SU
20,SU	**28,MO**
21,MO	**29, TU**
22,TU	**30, WE**
23,WE	

DECEMBER

"Let come what will, I mean to bear it out,
And either live with glorious victorie,
Or die with fame renown'd for chivalrie:
He is not worthy of the honey-comb,
That shuns the hives because the bees have stings"
Shakespeare

Honey, of course, allows bees to produce wax - and an enormous amount of it is needed for this task. This brings us back to the notes for January. Every scrap of wax must be saved including all that from old combs, whether from frames or top bars. To prevent the wax from being recycled for foundation, render it into blocks and use it for a range of products, from wax polishes to candles (see Ron Brown's excellent book: Beeswax - 3rd Edition, Revised, Published by Bee Books New and Old, 1995).

DAY	DECEMBER 2011 FORAGE	TEMP		WIND		CL'D	RAIN	1	2	3
		MIN	MAX	DIR	B.S			HIVE WEIGHT		
1										
2										
3										
4										
5										
6										
7										
8										
9										
10										
11										
12										
13										
14										
15										
16										
17										
18										
19										
20										
21										
22										
23										
24										
25										
26										
27										
28										
29										
30										
31										

DEC11

	8,TH
1,TH	9,FR
2,FR	10,SA ○ SR 07:54, SS 15:51
3,SA SR 07:45, SS 15:54	11,SU
4,SU	12,MO
5,MO	13,TU
6,TU	14,WE
7,WE ST AMBROSE DAY - PATRON SAINT OF BEEKEEPERS	15,TH

16,FR	24,SA ● SR 08:04, SS 15:55
17,SA SR 08:00, SS 15:51	25,SU CHRISTMAS DAY HOLIDAY
18,SU	**26,MO** BOXING DAY HOLIDAY
19,MO	**27,TU**
20,TU	**28,WE**
21,WE WINTER SOLSTICE	**29,TH**
22,TH	**30,FR**
23,FR	31,SA SR 08:06, SS 16:00

Hive/ Q NO.	Year Q Raised	Frames of Brood Autumn 2010	Combs Covered	Honey Stored- Sugar fed Kg	Combs Covered Spring 2011	Frames of Brood Spring 2011	Spring Feeding Kg	Queens Reared	Nuclei
1									
2									
3									
4									
5									
6									
7									
8									
9									
10									
11									
12									
13									
14									
15									
16									
17									
18									
19									
20									
21									
22									
23									
24									

HONEYBEE COLONIES

1									
2									
3									
4									
5									
6									
7									
8									
9									
10									
11									
12									
13									
14									
15									
16									
17									
18									
19									
20									
21									
22									
23									
24									

BEEEKEEPING RECORDS

Number	items	Est. Value £	P
	Stocks of Bees		
	Empty Hives		
	Combs - Deep - Shallow		
	Frames		
	Foundations		
	Honey Extractor		
	Honey Tanks		
	Other items		
	Honey Jars		
	Honey		

JANUARY 2012

S	M	T	W	T	F	S
1	2	3	4	5	6	7
8	9	10	11	12	13	14
15	16	17	18	19	20	21
22	23	24	25	26	27	28
29	30	31				

FEBRUARY 2012

S	M	T	W	T	F	S
			1	2	3	4
5	6	7	8	9	10	11
12	13	14	15	16	17	18
19	20	21	22	23	24	25
26	27	28	29			

MARCH 2012

S	M	T	W	T	F	S
				1	2	3
4	5	6	7	8	9	10
11	12	13	14	15	16	17
18	19	20	21	22	23	24
25	26	27	28	29	30	31

APRIL 2012

S	M	T	W	T	F	S
1	2	3	4	5	6	7
8	9	10	11	12	13	14
15	16	17	18	19	20	21
22	23	24	25	26	27	28
29	30					

MAY 2012

S	M	T	W	T	F	S
		1	2	3	4	5
6	7	8	9	10	11	12
13	14	15	16	17	18	19
20	21	22	23	24	25	26
27	28	29	30	31		

JUNE 2012

S	M	T	W	T	F	S
					1	2
3	4	5	6	7	8	9
10	11	12	13	14	15	16
17	18	19	20	21	22	23
24	25	26	27	28	29	30

JULY 2012

S	M	T	W	T	F	S
1	2	3	4	5	6	7
8	9	10	11	12	13	14
15	16	17	18	19	20	21
22	23	24	25	26	27	28
29	30	31				

AUGUST 2012

S	M	T	W	T	F	S
			1	2	3	4
5	6	7	8	9	10	11
12	13	14	15	16	17	18
19	20	21	22	23	24	25
26	27	28	29	30	31	

SEPTEMBER 2012

S	M	T	W	T	F	S
						1
2	3	4	5	6	7	8
9	10	11	12	13	14	15
16	17	18	19	20	21	22
23	24	25	26	27	28	29
30						

OCTOBER 2012

S	M	T	W	T	F	S
	1	2	3	4	5	6
7	8	9	10	11	12	13
14	15	16	17	18	19	20
21	22	23	24	25	26	27
28	29	30	31			

NOVEMBER 2012

S	M	T	W	T	F	S
				1	2	3
4	5	6	7	8	9	10
11	12	13	14	15	16	17
18	19	20	21	22	23	24
25	26	27	28	29	30	

DECEMBER 2012

S	M	T	W	T	F	S
						1
2	3	4	5	6	7	8
9	10	11	12	13	14	15
16	17	18	19	20	21	22
23	24	25	26	27	28	29
30	31					

All efforts have been made to ensure the accuracy of the information in these pages. Corrections and amendments should be sent to The Editor The Beekeepers Annual, c/o Northern Bee Books, Scout Bottom Farm, Mytholmroyd, Hebden Bridge HX7 5JS

DIRECTORY, ASSOCIATIONS AND SERVICES

DIRECTORY, ASSOCIATIONS AND SERVICES

BEEKEEPING MAILING LISTS

http://www.zbee.dircon.co.uk

Beekeeping mailing list services provided by zbee.com http://www.zbee.dircon.co.uk

KENT BEEKEEPERS ASSOCIATION, THE
Name of mailing list: Kentbee-L Serving a possible membership of 400. **Support website:** http://www.kentbee.com Approximately 80 have subscribed. Providing a forum for local branch announcements and news and chat about beekeeping. **To subscribe to Kentbee-L send a message to:** mailserver@zbee.com **Subject field:** You leave this blank it doesn't matter. **In the message body write:** Subscribe Kentbee-L then send the message and await further instructions to complete the subscription process.

NATIONAL HONEY SHOW, THE
Name of mailing list: NHS The National Honey Show is held in October each year in London, the support website http://www.honeyshow.co.uk has more information and schedules, **To subscribe to NHS send a message to:** mailserver@zbee.com, **Subject field:** You leave this blank it doesn't matter., **In the message body write:** Subscribe NHS then send the message and await further instructions to complete the subscription process

BEE IMPROVEMENT & BEE BREEDERS ASSOCIATION, THE (BIBBA)
Name of mailing list: BIBBA-L, Support website http://www.bibba.com/, **To subscribe to BIBBA-L send a message to:** mailserver@zbee.com, **Subject field:** You leave this blank it doesn't matter. **In the message body write:** Subscribe BIBBA-L then send the message and await further instructions to complete the subscription process.

APINET (BEEKEEPING EDUCATION EXTENSION NETWORK)
Name of mailing list: APINETL, Support website n/a, **To subscribe send a message to:** mailserver@zbee.com, **Subject field:** You leave this blank it doesn't matter.
In the message body write: Subscribe APINETL then send the message and await further instructions to complete the subscription process.

BROMLEY & SIDCUP & ORPINGTON BEEKEEPERS ASSOCIATION
Name of mailing list: BBK, **Support website:** http://www.kentbee.com/, **To subscribe to BBK send a message to:** mailserver@zbee.com, **Subject field:** You leave this blank it doesn't matter. **In the message body write:** Subscribe BBK then send the message and await further instructions to complete the subscription process.

THE BRITISH BEEKEEPERS ASOCIATION (BBKA)
Name of mailing list: BBKA, **Support website:** http://www.bbka.org.uk, Private list members only, see members area for joining details.

APIS-UK
The monthly beekeeping magazine, edited by David Cramp and sent directly to your computer. To subscribe go to www.beedata.com and click on the Apis-UK link..

BEE DISEASES INSURANCE LTD

SECRETARY
Donald Robertson-Adams
Bryngwrog
Beulah, Newcastle Emlyn
Ceredigion, SA38 9QR
01239 711782
member@theoldmill.fsnet.co.uk

TREASURER AND SCHEME B MANAGER
Mrs Sharon Blake
Stratton Court,
South Petherton,
Somerset TA13 5LQ
01460 242124
m-s.blake@overstratton.fsnet.co.uk

CLAIMS MANAGER
Bernard Diaper
57 Marfield Close,
Walmley,
Sutton Coldfield B76 1YD
0121 3133112
b.diaper@tiscali.co.uk

PRESIDENT
Richard Ball
Stoneyford Farmhouse
Colaton Raleigh
Sidmouth
Devon, EX10 0HZ
01395 567990
richard.ball@fera.gsi.gov.uk

Bee Diseases Insurance (BDI) provides insurance cover for individual beekeepers, association apiaries and commercial beekeepers alike, against the possibility of their bees and equipment being destroyed as a result of a Destruction Order following a visit from an authorised Bee Inspector. .

BDI provides compensation for specified property that may need to be destroyed as a result of American Foul Brood and European Foul Brood.

BDI has established a contingency fund capped at £25,000 a year if Small Hive Beetle or Tropilaelaps infestation is found.

Scheme A provides cover for the beekeeper with a total of 39 colonies or less. Cover is obtained by being a member of a Beekeeping Association that is a member of BDI Ltd.

Scheme B provides cover for beekeepers with 40 or more colonies in total. Insurance under this Scheme is on a personal basis and further details can be obtained from the Scheme B Manager.

REMEMBER: DISEASE CAN STRIKE ANY COLONY AT ANY TIME AND IT IS SPREAD THROUGHOUT THE COUNTRY. PROTECT YOUR APIARY THROUGH B.D.I.

BEE FARMERS' ASSOCIATION OF THE UNITED KINGDOM

The BFA represents the professional beekeepers of the UK.

The association is the largest contract pollinator in the UK and our members are responsible for virtually all the migratory pollination. They are expected to have a good degree of competence; membership requires over 40 hives, and sponsorship by a BFA member who knows the applicant as a beekeeper. We have recently introduced a code of conduct which members are expected to observe. In addition we have a significant number of members who get some income from being bee inspectors, responsible for identifying and dealing with notifiable disease.

We have one business meeting a year which follows the Annual General Meeting in April at Stoneleigh on the same Saturday as the BBKA convention. Business is also conducted at twice-yearly regional meetings which pass items up to the main meeting for discussion and voting, and which put forward candidates for the committee.

The BFA is affiliated to the National Farmers Union and The Honey (Packers) Association with whom we work effectively in promoting ecological sensitive farming and in promoting consumer awareness through events such 'National Honey Week' and bulk sales to retail chains.

MEMBERSHIP

Our members are expected to have a good degree of competence.

FULL MEMBERSHIP requires over 40 hives, and sponsorship by a BFA member who knows the applicant as a beekeeper.

ASSOCIATE MEMBERSHIP is a stepping stone to full membership of the BFA for beekeepers with a minimum of 20 hives and who would like to take up commercial or semi-commercial beekeeping.

Membership forms are available from the Membership Secretary, or as a download from our website.

FUNCTIONS

- To monitor and to keep members informed about developments in commercial beekeeping, bee science

CHAIRMAN, John Home
Northcote
Deppers Bridge
Southam,
Warwickshire
CV47 2SU
01926 612 322
northcote4home@
btinternet.com

VICE CHAIRMAN,
Robin Lewis
4 Meadow View,
Llanfihangel,
Talyllyn,
Brecon.
LD3 7TX
01874 658466

TREASURER,
Mr. D. Isles
Hudnalls Apiary
The Hudnalls, St Briavels
Lydney Gloucestershire
GL15 5RT
dougisles@yahoo.co.uk

SECRETARY, J. Howat
8 Olivers Close
West Totton
Southampton SO40 8FH
02380 907850
02380 907850
john@eclipse01.
demon.co.uk

POLLINATION SEC,
Alan Hart
61 Fakenham Road,
Great Witchingham,
Norwich,
NORFOLK
NR9 5AE
01603 308911
earlswoodbees@hotmail.co.uk

BULLETIN EDITOR,
David Bancalari
Park Farm Barn
Shortthorn Road
Stratton Strawless
Norfolk
NR10 5NX
David@Bancalari.fslife.co.uk

MEMBERSHIP SECRETARY
Gerry Fry
2, The Glade,
Waterlooville
Hants
PO7 7PD
02392 520075
gerry_fry@sky.com

and UK and EEC legislation.

- Liaison with Farmers, Growers, Contractors, Consumers and other organisations.
- Liaison with UK Government Departments dealing with beekeeping, medicines, and allied matters.
- Liaison and co-operation with UK Beekeeping organisations.
- Contact with European beekeeping organisations (EPBA) and representation on the EEC Honey Working Party (COPA/COGECA) in Brussels.
- Political lobbying through MPs and Euro MPs.
- Member of the Confederation of National Beekeeping Associations (CONBA)
- Member of the European Professional Beekeepers' Association (EPBA)
- Associate member of the Honey Association

FACILITIES FOR MEMBERS:

- Bi-monthly Bulletins with news and updates, notes on meetings with DEFRA, FERA, VMD, and the EEC, reports on current beekeeping problems (e.g. varroa) and commercial developments world-wide.. This bulletin is available as a paper and/or an e-document
  *e-news. Frequent electronic updates on news items
- Free advertisement of members' sales and wants (including hive products, bee stocks and spare equipment).
* Regional meetings which provide for local discussion and opportunities for trading between members.
- Crop and winter loss reports.
- Free Circulation among members of UK and foreign magazines.
- Free insurance for products and third party liability (not limited to thirty hives).
- Special rates for employers liability insurance.
- Comprehensive special beefarmers insurance with the NFU.
- Pollination contracts.
- Advice from experienced members on all aspects of honey farming and commercial beekeeping; sources of equipment and sundries.
- Product directory listing specialist suppliers.
- Discounts from suppliers.
- Bulk purchase schemes to minimize costs to individual members..

ANNUAL CONVENTION WEEKEND

- Spring meeting for members and partners, held each March at different locations in the UK or abroad. Visits to local bee and research establishments; lectures and discussions on bee-related matters; sight seeing, and social events.

In 2011 our Conference will be at the South Devon coast

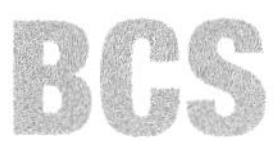

BEEKEEPING COURSES & SERVICES

PART TIME LECTURERS & FURTHER EDUCATION COURSES IN BEEKEEPING

The following may offer a range of theoretical and practical courses in beekeeping, in some cases an advisory service or a diagnostic service for adult bee diseases only may be offered.

The range of services and activities is wide and this list is not exhaustive but the following may be contacted for details of facilities in an enquirer's area.

BEDFORDSHIRE,
Mike Nieman
43 Flitwick Road
Westoning
Bedfordshire
MK45 5JA
01525 717040
Harry Inman
10 Constable Hill
Bedford
MK41 7LJ
01234 306554
* Beekeeping for Beginners
* Practical Beekeeping

BERKSHIRE COLLEGE OF AGRICULTURE, Kate Malenczuk and Reg Hook
Hall Place,
Burchetts Green
Maidenhead,
Berkshire SL6 6QR
www.bca.ac.uk
01628 824444
fax, 01628 827488
- Beekeeping for beginners
- Practical Beekeeping
- Preparing Bees for Winter
- Intermediate Beekeeping
- Taster Sessions

CHESHIRE BEEKEEPERS (STOCKPORT BRANCH)
- Introduction To Beekeeping Course,
- Practical Beekeeping,

Stockport :-
Mrs Carolin Hallworth
01625 875 436
North Cheshire (Frodsham):-
Dan Fox 01565 777 341
South Cheshire (Bradwall):-
Mrs Liz Camm 01270 664 337
Wirral
Doug Jones (Thornton Hough)
0151 342 7062

DEVON, Dr. Mick Street
c/o Bicton College
Budleigh Salterton
EX9 7BY
or the DBKA Education Officer at;
www.devonbeekeepers.co.uk

ESSEX, Richard Ridler
Treasurer,
C/O Saffron Walden Division,
Essex Beekeepers' Association,
Rundle House,
High Street
Hatfield Brand Oak,
Bishop's Stortford
Hertfordshire
CM22 7HE
richard.ridler@uwclub.net
01279 718111
07942 815753

LEEDS
For Details See YBKA

NORFOLK, Paul Metcalf NDB
Easton College, Easton
Norwich NR9 8DX

SUSSEX, Business Training
Plumpton College
Ditchling Road
Plumpton, Nr Lewes
East Sussex BN7 3AE
pd@plumpton.ac.uk

STOCKPORT (see Cheshire)

WILTSHIRE,The Secretary
Melksham Beekeepers Association
Deans End
Butts Lane
Keevil,
Trowbridge
BA14 6LZ
wickhamsoftkeevil@btinternet.com

YBKA, Bill Cadmore,
104 Hall Lane, Horsforth
Leeds LS18 5JG
0113 216 0482
bill.cadmore@ntlworld.com
Venue:
Home Farm Rare Breeds Centre
Temple Newsam House
Garden & Estate East Leeds

BEEKEEPING EDITORS' EXCHANGE SCHEME

BEES is a self-help grouping of local, county and country beekeeping association editors, which operates principally by exchanging journals through a central address. The scheme is supported by Northern Bee Books.

BEES was founded in 1984 and for many years has been an exchange of paper copy. However, the focus has now changed to an electronic exchange, using the server of one of the participating editors.

Now fully established as part of the British and Irish beekeeping scene, the scheme brings up to date information to beekeepers throughout the British Isles.

The aims are:

- to exchange ideas for content and production methods
- to aid others by experience
- to communicate matters editorial
- to share information on national beekeeping issues
- to help and reassure those new to the task
- to give a wider readership to the best writing in beekeeping journalism

If you are an editor or potential editor and would like to know more about how we operate write to Martin Robinson.
The Manor House, Blackshaw Head, Hebden Bridge HX7 7JR
01422 - 842794

CONTACT,
Chris Jackson
22 Chapter Close
Oakwood
Derby
DE21 2BG

B.E.E.S
Helping Editors
Help Themselves

Sponsored by
NORTHERN BEE BOOKS

BEES ABROAD UK Ltd

Supporting beekeeping projects overseas

ADMINISTATOR
MRS JULES MOORE
PO BOX 2058
BRISTOL
BS35 9AF
0207 7193 7135
info@beesabroad.org.uk

Bees Abroad is a UK-registered charity (No 1108464) which was established in 1999. Its principle aim is the relief of poverty in the developing world using beekeeping and associated skills as a tool of individual, group and community empowerment for poverty alleviationand to provide sustainable income. Beekeeping is a valuable tool as it is socially and culturally acceptable for both genders across a wide age range.It can cost very little to set up a beekeeping operation, which will deliver benefits for income, education, health, environment and community. Beekeeping and its associated skills deliver access to gainful self-emplyment for poor and disadvantaged groups. This enables them to recover social status, improve social interactions, obtain income and aquire new skills to build the confidence to represent their own interests. Bees Abroad receives a high volume of direct appeals for assistance from groups all over the world. In practice, it acheives its aims through a volunteer network of supporters, committee members and project managers.Bees Abroad takes care to ensure that its projects are sustainable and not dependent on constant external input. This is done by supporting community group initiatives, setting up village-based field extension services, running training courses for beekeeping trainers and financing local trainers' wages. All Bees Abroad projects are designed to become self-financing after a defines time period, usually 2-3 years, but sometimes longer. Its first two projects in Nepal and Cameroon now employ 42 beekeeper trainers and involve many more. It currently has projects either runnung or seeking funding in Malawi, Kenya, Ghana, Nepal, Uganda and Nigeria.

Our committee is almost entirely run by volunteers, who are all beekeepers. Volunteers and members currently undertake all activities, including fundraising, though a part-time administrator is employed for one day a week. We also arrange Beekeeping Holidays to variety of locations, including Chile, Cameroon and Kenya.
For more details of what we do and how you can help, you can contact Mrs Jules Moore the Administrator, Bees Abroad. Membership costs £15.00 per annum.

BEES FOR DEVELOPMENT TRUST

(UK Registered Charity 1078803)

www.beesfordevelopment.org

CONTACT, Dr Nicola Bradbear
Bees for Development
PO Box 105, Monmouth,
NP25 9AA
Tel 016007 13648

E-mail. info@beesfordevelopment.org
Web www.beesfordevelopment.org

PLEASE SUPPORT BEES FOR DEVELOPMENT

Ways you can help

- ☐ Subscribe to Bees for Development Journal
- ☐ Sponsor a subscription and encourage your Association to do likewise
- ☐ Give a donation
- ☐ Join one of our Safaris
- ☐ Buy our special labels and tamper proof seals for your honey jars and bee products
- ☐ Buy your bee reading and viewing from us

Bees for Development works to provide information to beekeepers in developing countries where reliable apicultural information is hard to find. We advocate beekeeping as an effective way for people to create income from natural resources without damaging them. We respond to 4,000 enquiries that arrive by e-mail and post from beekeepers in developing countries each year.

Our work

Bees for Development Journal: Enjoyed by readers in over 100 countries, our Journal keeps everyone in our network in touch. 95% of recipients cannot afford to pay a subscription and therefore we seek funding to sponsor them. We are assisted in this significant task by our charity Bees for Development Trust.

Project management: current examples - Bees, people and forest biodiversity in South India; Increasing honey trade in Uganda; Investigating beekeeping potential to assist subsistence farmers in southern Sudan.

Expert advice: We assist enquirers from developing countries without charging a fee. For those living elsewhere we make a nominal charge.

Beekeepers' Safaris: Friendly holidays run in co-operation with our overseas partners.

Beekeeping books, videos, CDs and posters: see our comprehensive web store.

Training courses, study tours and symposia and presentations about our work.

BRITISH BEEKEEPERS' ASSOCIATION www.britishbee.org.uk

COMMITTEES OF THE EXECUTIVE AND SECRETARIES

FINANCE COMMITTEE

The Finance Committee reviews and agrees budgets and deals with issues relating to insurance, investments and setting the proposals for capitation etc. It acts as a co-ordinator for all external fund raising.

EDUCATION & HUSBANDRY

The Education and Husbandry Committee develops practical guidance on beekeeping, produces advisory leaflets on husbandry topics, liaises with the Examination Board to develop training materials to support Area Association tutors.

EXAMINATIONS BOARD

Secretary: Mrs Val Francis
val.francis@bbka.org.uk

The Examinations Board of the BBKA performs a national function, providing a structured range of examinations fulfilling the needs of all beekeepers. All matters concerning examinations, except for the correspondence course, should be addressed to the Examination Secretary.

PRODUCTS AND PROMOTIONS

The Products and Promotions Committee seeks ways to promote bees and beekeeping at both local and national level. It monitors media coverage and ensures that BBKA contributes to any relevant debate.

GENERAL SECRETARY
National Beekeeping Centre
NAC, Stoneleigh Park
Warwickshire CV8 2LG
024 7669 6679
Fax: 024 7669 0682
generalsecretary@britishbeekeepers.com

BRITISH BEEKEEPERS ASSOCIATION
National Beekeeping Centre
Stoneleigh Park, Stoneleigh
Warks CV8 2LG
02476 696679
Fax: 024 7669 0682
Office hours 9.00am–5.00 pm Monday - Friday (inclusive)
Telephone answering service outside office hours
bbka@britishbeekeepers.com

EXECUTIVE COMMITTEE

PRESIDENT
Martin Smith
martin.smith@bbka.org.uk

CHAIRMAN
Brian Ripley
brian.ripley@bbka.org.uk

VICE CHAIRMAN
David Aston
david.aston@bbka.org.uk

TREASURER
Michael Sheasby
michael.sheasby@bbka.org.uk

ENVIRONMENTAL AND TECHNICAL

The Environmental and Technical Committee monitors technical developments and assesses their potential impact on bees and beekeeping.

SUBSCRIPTIONS AND MEMBERSHIP FEES

Individual membership fees for direct membership of the BBKA are now £18 for an overseas member or £33 per annum for UK members. All other membership is through local Area Associations.

LEGAL ADVICE

The Legal Adviser to the BBKA may be able to help Local Associations with legal problems to a limited extent. Contact through the NBC, BBKA, Stoneleigh Park, Kenilworth, CV8 2LG.

EVENTS

The various gatherings of beekeepers continue to be a feature of BBKA's many functions and provide a vital service for the dissemination of knowledge.

BBKA SPRING CONVENTION

The Spring Convention at Stoneleigh is now a firmly established major event focussing on lectures, workshops and trade stands.

OTHER NATIONAL EVENTS

The BBKA has stands featuring bees and promoting beekeeping at a number of national agricultural and garden shows throughout the year.

INSURANCE

Members and Area Associations and its Branches/ Divisions are indemnified against claims for Public Liability and Product Liability to a limit of £5 million. Each new claim carries an excess of £500 payable by the member.

Also available is the 'All Risks' Insurance for Associations which is available on request for use by Associations to cover the loss or damage to an Association's property or equipment. The terms of the policy are flexible and can be discussed with the broker.

Further details can be obtained from the BBKA Treasurer.

PUBLICATIONS

- The BBKA Year Book contains detailed information about the BBKA. including the Annual Accounts. Copies can may be purchased from the BBKA, Stoneleigh Park, Kenilworth, CV8 2LG.
- BBKA News is issued six times a year and is free to all members of BBKA. The Editor is Mrs. S. Blake. sharon.blake@bbka.org.uk
- A Directory of Lecturers & Demonstrators is included in the Year Book.

BBKA ENTERPRISES LIMITED

BBKA Enterprises Ltd is a private company limited by guarantee with all profits from the trading activities being donated to the BBKA. The company offers a range of beekeeping, corporate and related items, specially selected gifts, travel items and educational material. Recent additions to the range include the Gold Medal winning 'Healthy Hive Guide'. Visit the BBKA website for illustrations and details of prices. www.britishbee.org.uk or contact BBKA Enterprises Ltd, NBC, Stoneleigh Park, Kenilworth, CV8 2LG   02476 696679.

BBKA WEBSITE

The BBKA Website contains technical information, is easy to navigate and focuses on new beekeepers. You can download publications, find help and advice in the discussion forums, purchase merchandise, access the members' area, the Bees4kids section, download BBKA exam application forms and the exam syllabus. Associations can promote their beekeeping events and have links to association websites.

TRUSTEE MEMBERS

SLIDE AND VIDEO LIBRARY

A comprehensive catalogue of the BBKA Slide and VHS Video Library is available from Bridget Knutson, the Librarian at £1.80 including P&P. The slides are 35mm, both colour and B&W; some are supported with lecture notes. Many sets are now available as Power Point presentations, please enquire.

We are always pleased to receive suggestions for new additions to our range and for donations of items to improve the service. Please contact Mrs Bridget Knutson bridget_knutson@yahoo.co.uk

AREA ASSOCIATION SECRETARIES

AVON, Jane Godwin
Chatleigh house
6 Warminster Road
Limley Stoke
Bath
BA2 7GD
01225 723292
janegoodwin@macace.net

BERKSHIRE, Martin Moore,
19 Armour Hill
Tilehurst
READING
RG31 6JP
01189677386
07729620286
secretary.berksbees@uwclub.net

BOURNEMOUTH
Mr A Curry
40 Lacy Drive,
Wimbourne, BW21 1DG
01202 840993
andrew@curry@virgin.net

BUCKS, Dr Beulah Cullen
26 Sweetcroft Lane,
Uxbridge, UB10 9LD,
01895 234704
beulah.cullen@virgin.net

CAMBRIDGESHIRE
Mrs Judith Evans MBE
7 The Furlongs
Needingworth
St Ives
Cambridgeshire PE27 4TX
01480 461203
judith@evans.cambnset.co.uk

CHESHIRE, M.F. Haynes
98, Gatley Road, Gatley,
Cheadle,
Cheshire SK8 4AB
0161 491 2382
thesecretary@cheshire-bka.co.uk

CHESTERFIELD, Robin Bagnall
21 Ramper Avenue,
Clowne, Chesterfield
Derbyshire S43 4UD
01246 570545
ancient.mariner74-79@virgin.net

CORNWALL, Julia Cooper
Whistow Farm, Lanlivery,
Bodmin, PL30 5DE
01208 872865
julia.i.cooper@btinternet.com

CORNWALL WEST
Mrs Berenice Robbins
Dr Anne McQuade,
5 Trevellan Road, Mylor
Bridge, Falmouth
Cornwall, TR11 5NE
01326 373749

CUMBRIA, Stephen C Barnes
8 Albemarle Street
Cockermouth
Cumbria CA13 0BG
01900 824872
braithwaitebees@sky.com

DERBYSHIRE, M J Cross
Harlestone, Beggarswell
Wood, Ambergate
Derbyshire DE56 2HF
01773 852772
crosssk@btinternet.com

DEVON, Andrew Kyle
62 Bicton Street,
Exmouth EX8 2RU
01395 263509
andrewkyle@tiscali.co.uk

DORSET, Mrs Ruth Homer
5, Malters Cottage,
Litton Cheney,
Dorchester DT2 9AE
beekeepers@hotmail.com

DOVER & DISTRICT
Mrs Maggie Harrowell
4 Harton Cottages, Ashley,
Dover, CT15 5HS
01304 821208
the.harrowells@btinternet.com

DURHAM, John Metson
7 Sidegate, Durham City,
Durham
0191 384 5170

ESSEX, Mrs Pat Allen
8 Frank's Cottages
St Mary's Lane
Upminster RM14 3NU
01708 220897
pat.allen@btconnect.com

GLOUCESTERSHIRE
Marie Toman
Oak Cottage,
Stoulgrove Lane, Woodcroft,
Chepstow, Mon., NP16 7QE.
01291 620345
marietoman@btconnect.com

GWENT
Mrs J Bromley
Ty Hir, Monmouth Road
Raglan, Usk. NP15 2ET
01291 690331
bromleyjan@hotmail.com

HAMPSHIRE, Mrs P Barker
Brookdean, Hillbrow
Liss, Hampshire GU33 7PT
01730 895368
H'GATE & RIPON
Mr Frank Ward
19 High Street
Starbeck, Harrogate
HG2 7NS
01423 880266
HEREFORDSHIRE
Mrs. Wendy Cummins
Brook Cottage
Whitbourne
Worcsestershire WR6 5RT
01886 821485
jerryandwendy@btinternet.com
HERTFORDSHIRE
Luke Adams
53 Park Street Lane
Park Street
St. Albans
Hertfordshire AL2 2JA
01442 843 779
luke.skywalker@virgin.net
HUNTINGDON,
Nick Steiger
Bull Cottage, Main Street,
Upton, Huntingdon, Cambs,
PE28 5YB
01480 891935
n.steiger@btinternet.com
ISLE OF MAN,
Janet Thompson
Cott ny Greiney, The Smelt,
Beach Road, Port St Mary,
Isle of Man, IM9 5NF
01624 835524
jthompson@manx.net

ISLE OF WIGHT,
Mrs. Mary Case
Limerstone Farm
Limerstone,
Newport
Isle of White PO404AB
01983 759510
KENDAL &
SOUTH WESTMORLAND
Roger Blocksidge
Castle Garden Cottage
Aynam Road, Kendal
Cumbria LA9 7DE
01539 734436
tinky_winky@hotmail.com
KENT, John D. Hendrie
26 Coldharbour Lane
Hildenborough, Tonbridge
Kent TN11 9JT
01732 833894
jdh@bbka.freeserve.co.uk
LANCASHIRE & NORTH WEST
Martin Smith
137 Blaguegate Lane,
Lathom
Skelmersdale
Wigan WN8 8TX
05601 484388
ormskirk_beekeepers@
hotmail.com
LINCOLNSHIRE
Mrs. Celia Smith
Brookfield, Moor Town Road,
Nettleton LN7 6HX
01472 851165
LONDON
Nikki Vane
601 Alaska, 61 Grange Road
London SE1 3BB
07909 964986
sec@lbka.org.uk

LUDLOW & DIST
Andy M Vanderbrook
The Old Forge
Baveney Wood
Cleobury Mortimer
Kidderminster
DY14 8JD
01299 841379
andy.vanderhook@
care4free.net
MANCH. & DIST, Mrs. M. Bohme
54 Dunster Drive, Flixton
Manchester M41 6WR
0161 747 7292
MEDWAY Mrs. M. Pines
26 Lapwing Road
Isle of Grain, Rochester
ME3 0EB
01634 272252
MIDDLESEX, Mrs. J.V. Telfer
Midwood House
Elm Park Road
Pinner HA5 3LH
020 8868 3494
jvtelfer@hotmail.com
NEWCASTLE & DISTRICT,
Mr D Varty
Cragside, Dipton
Stan DH9 9EL
01207 570229
NORFOLK, Mrs H Coppwaite
1 The Maltings, Millgate
Aylsham, Norwich
NR11 6GX
01263 734682
NORFOLK WEST & KINGS LYNN
Mrs Irene Laws
16 Pine Road,
South Wootton
King's Lynn PE30 3JP
01553 671312

NORTHAMPTONSHIRE
Mrs Ruth Stewart
17 Leys Avenue, Rothwell,
Kettering,
Northants, NN14 6JF
01536 507293
rstewart@euramax.co.uk
NORTHUMBERLAND
Mr Ben Hopkinson
11 Watershaugh Rd
Warkworth, Northumberland
NE65 0TT
01665 714213
benhopkinson2436@waitrose.com
NOTTINGHAMSHIRE
M. Jordan
29 Crow Park Avenue
Sutton on Trent
Nr Newark NG23 6QG
01636 821613
mauricejordan11@btinternet.com
OXFORDSHIRE, Mr Mark Lynch
71 Millwood End Long
Hanborough
Oxfordshire, OX 29 8BP
01993 883266
marka_lynch@hotmail.com
PETERBOROUGH & DISTRICT
P George Newton
65 Queen Street, Yaxley
Peterborough PE7 7JE
01733 243349
ROSELAND BEEKEEPING GROUP
Rose Hardisty
Menagwins Cottage,
Pentewan Road, St Austell,
Cornwall PL26 7AN
01726 74101
roselandbee@tiscali.co.uk
SEDBURGH
Jane Callus-Whitton
Harren House, Woodman
Lane, Cowan Bridge,
Carnforth, LA6 2HT
01524 272004
SHROPSHIRE
Mrs Penny Carkeet-James
Upper Dumble Holes
Westbury
Shrewsbury SY5 9HE
01743 791081
SHROPSHIRE NORTH
Mrs Jo Schup
Fields Farm, Malt Kiln Lane
Dobsons Bridge,
Whixall SY13 2QL
01948 720731
SOMERSET,
Mrs S Perkins
Tengore House,
Tengore Lane, Langport
Somerset TA10 9JL
01458 250095
bernieperkns.tengor@tiscali.co.uk
STAFFORDSHIRE NORTH
Janey Hayward
90 Ostler's Lane
Cheddleton ST13 7HS
01538 361048
STAFFORDSHIRE SOUTH
Mr Steve Halford
46 Lincoln Hill Telford
TF8 7QA
01952 432031
stevehal@tiscali.co.uk
STRATFORD-ON-AVON
Michael Osborne
Oak Lodge, King's Lane
Snitterfield
Stratford-upon-Avon
Warwickshire CV37 0RB
01789 731745
mjroosborne@btinternet.com
SUFFOLK,
Ian McQueen
643 Foxhall Road
Ipswich IP3 8NE
01473 420187
jackie.mcqueen@ntlworld.com
SURREY, Mrs Sandra Rick
19 Kenwood Drive,
Walton-on-Thames
Surrey. KT12 5AU
01932 244 326
rickwoodsbka@googlemail.com
SUSSEX, Mrs Moyra Davidson
Gainsborough Cottage, Stunts
Green, Hertsmonceux,
East Sussex, BN27 4PN
01323 831 650
secretary@sussexbee.org.uk
SUSSEX WEST,
Mr John Glover
Fletchings Hollow
Vicarage Hill, Loxwood,
West Sussex RH14 0RJ
01403 751 899
glover.fletchershollow@googlemail.com
THANET,
Mrs R Pearce
Summerfield Cottage
Summerfield
Woodnesborough
Nr Sandwich CT13 0EW
01304 614789

TWICKENHAM & THAMES VALLEY (MOLE APIARY CLUB)
Mrs Sarah Crofton
11 Wellesley Avenue
London TW3 2PB
0208 222 8216

WARWICKSHIRE,
Theresa Simkin
87 Kineton Green Road
Solihull, B92 7DT
secretary@
warwickshirebeekeepers.org.uk

WILTSHIRE,
Ruth Woodhouse
Sandridge Tower
Bromham
Devizes
SN15 2JN
01225 705382
sandridgetower@aol.com

WORCESTERSHIRE
Mr Chris Broad, Upper
Gambolds Farm, Upper
Gambolds Lane, Stoke Prior,
B60 2DF
01527 872448

WYE VALLEY, Mrs S Wenczek
Hopleys, Bearwood
Leominster HR6 8EQ
01544 388302

YORKSHIRE, Brian Latham
111 Woodland Road
Whitkirk, Leeds
LS15 7DN
0113 264 3436
chrisbroad1964@btinternet.
com

ASSOCIATION EXAMINATION SECRETARIES

AVON, Position Vacant
Please contact
Hon. General Secretary
Julie Young
01179 372 156

BERKSHIRE,
Mrs Rosemary Bayliss
Norbury, Coppid Beech Hill,
Binfield, Berkshire.
RG42 4BS
01344 421747

BOURNEMOUTH, Mrs. M. Davies
80 Leybourne Avenue
Ensbury Park
Bournemouth
Dorset BH10 6HE
01202 526077

BUCKS, John Chudley
Orchard Lea, Oxford Street
Lea Common
Great Missenden HP16 9JT
01494 837544
jlchudley@tiscali.co.uk

CHESHIRE
Graham Royle NDB,
7, Symondley Road,
Sutton,
Macclesfield. SK11 0HT
01260 252 042

CORNWALL
Mrs. Susan Malcolm
Fig Tree, 333 New Road
Saltash, Cornwall
PL12 6HL
01752 845496

DEVON, Roger Lacey
Gatchell House
Toadpit Lane, Ottery St Mary
Devon EX11 1TR
01404 811733
devonbees@pobox.com

DORSET, K.G.Bishop
72 Alexandra Road
Bridport DT6 5AL
01308 425479

DURHAM, G. Eames
23 Lancashire Drive
Belmont, Durham,
DH1 2DE
01913 845220
george.eames@durham.ac.uk

ESSEX, Pat Allan
8, Frank's Cottages
St. Mary's Lane
Upminster, RM14 3NU
pat.allen@btconnect.com

GLOUCESTERSHIRE
Bernard Danvers
120a Ruspidge Road
Cinderford,
Glocestershire
GL143AG
01594 825063

GWENT, Mrs J Bromley
Ty Hir, Monmouth Road
Raglan, Usk. NP15 2ET
01291 690331
bromleyjan@hotmail.com

HAMPSHIRE, Mrs Peggy Mason
37 Springford Crescent
Lordswood,
SO16 5LF
023 8077 7705

H'GATE & RIPON, Peter Ross
The Wheelhouse, The Green,
Old Scriven, Knaresborough
HG5 9EA, 01423 866565,
pjeross@btinternet.com

HEREFORDSHIRE, Len J. Dixon
The Square, Titley,
Kington
Herefordshire HR5 3RG
01544 230884
beeline2ljd@yahoo.co.uk

HERTFORDSHIRE, R. E. A. Dartington
15 Benslow Lane
Hitchin SG4 9RE
01462 450707
gray.dartington@dial.pipex.com

ISLE OF WIGHT, Mrs M. Case
Limerstone Farm,
Limerstone, Newport,
Isle of Wight, PO30 4AB
01983 740223
gcase90337@aol.com

KENT, P. F. W. Hutton
22 Good Station Road
Tunbridge Wells,
TN1 2DB
01892 530688

LANCASHIRE & NW
Edward Hill
3 Sandy Lane, Aughton
Ormskirk
L39 6SL
01695 423137

LEICESTERSHIRE & RUTLAND
Brian Cramp
2 Woodland Drive, Groby
Leicester
LE6 0BQ
01162 876879

LINCOLNSHIRE, R. J. B. Hickling
Linden Lea, Sandbraes
Lane, Caistor, LN7 6SB
01472 851473

MIDDLESEX
Mrs Jo V Telfer
Midwood House
Elm Park Road, Pinner
Middlesex HA5 3LH
020 8868 3494
e-mail, jvtelfer@hotmail.com

NOTTINGHAMSHIRE
Dr Glyn D Flowerdew
Knight Cross Cottage
Newstead Abbey Park
Ravenshead
Nottinghamshire NG15 8GE
01623 792812

OXFORDSHIRE, Terry. Thomas
4 Kirk Close
Oxford, OX2 8JN
01865 558679

PETERBOROUGH, P. G .Newton
65 Queen Street, Yaxley
Peterborough PE7 3JE
01733 243349

SHROPSHIRE NORTH
Paul Curtis
1 Hammer Close
Overton-on-Dee, Wrexham
Clwyd LL13 0LD0
01691 624296

SOMERSET, Mrs Angela Bache
Greenway House
Badgers Cross
Somerton TA11 7JB
Tel 01458 273149

STAFFS.Nth Dr. Nick C Mawby
Glenwood, Wood Lane
Longsdon,
Stoke on Trent ST9 9QB
01538 387506
info@northstaffsbees.org.uk

STAFFS. SOUTH
Tony Burton
96 Weeping Cross, Stafford,
Staffordshire. ST9 9QB
01538 399322

SUFFOLK, Mr Ian McQueen
643 Foxhall Road, Ipswich,
Suffolk, IP3 8NE
01473 420187

SURREY, Mrs. A. Gill
143 Smallfield Road
Horley, RH6 9LR
01293 784161

SUSSEX, Nigel Champion
45 Ridgeway,
Hurst Green
Etchingham
East Sussex TN19 7PJ
01580 860379

SUSSEX WEST
Mrs A. S. Gibson-Poole
Mont Dore, West Hill
High Salvington
Worthing, BN13 3BZ
01903 260914

TWICKENHAM, Chris Deaves
12 Chatsworth Crescent
Hounslow,
Middlesex
TW3 2PB
0208 5682869
e-mail,
c-deavs@compuserve.com

WARWICKSHIRE, P.D. Lishman
Aston Farm House
Newtown Lane
Shustoke, ColeshillB46 2SD
01676 540411

WILTSHIRE, John Troke
The Lythe
Hop Gardens
Whiteparish, Salisbury,
Wiltshire SP5 2SS
01373 822892

WORCHESTERSHIRE, D.P. Friel
17 Tennal Rd, Harborne
Birmingham, B32 2JD
0121 427 1211

YORKSHIRE, D. R. Gue
87 Grove Park
Beverley, HU17 9JU
01482 881288

Where Associations have no Examinations Secretary the Association Secretary deals with examinations. To help future candidates it is suggested that Associations without an Examination Secretary appoint one. Associations are responsible for arranging a suitable room for the written examinations and recommending an invigilator.

If you live in an area without a nominated Exam Secretary, you should contact Mrs Val Frances, 39 Beevor Lane, Gawber, Barnsley, S75 2RP Tel 01226 286341. e-mail, valfrances@blueyonder.co.uk

HOLDERS OF THE BBKA SENIOR JUDGES CERTIFICATE

ASHLEY, Mr. T. E.
Meadow Cottage
Elton Lane, Winterley
Sandbach
Cheshire CW11 4TN

BADGER, M.J , MBE
14 Thorn Lane
Leeds, LS8 1NN

BLACKBURN, Mrs. H.M
15 Highdown Hill Road
Emmer Green
Reading RG4 8QR

BROWN, Mrs. V

BUCKLE, M.J
The Little House
Newton Blossomville
Bedford MK43 8AS
01234 881262
martin@newtonbee.fsnet.co.uk

CAPENER, Rev. H.F.
1 Baldric Road
Folkestone CT20 2NR

COLLINS, G.M. , NDB
72 Tatenhill Gardens
Doncaster DN4 6TL

COOPER, Miss R.M
10 Gaskells End
Tokers Green
Reading RG4 9EW

DAVIES, Mrs. M
80 Leybourne Avenue
Ensbury Park
Bournemouth BH10 6HE

DIAPER, B
B Diaper
57 Marfield Close
Walmley
Sutton Coldfield
West Midlands
0121 313 3112

DICKSON, Ms. F
Didlington Manor
Didlington, Thetford
Norfolk IP26 5AT

DUFFIN, J.M
Upper Hurst
Salisbury Road, Blashford
Ringwood
Hampshire BH24 3PB
01425 474552

DUGGAN, R.M
Redstone Wood Cottage
Philanthropic Lane
Redhill RH1 4DF

FIELDING, L.G
Linley, Station Road
Lichfield WS13 6HZ

MacGIOLLA COSA, M.C.
Glengarra Wood, Burncourt
Cahir, Co. Tipperary
Republic of Ireland

McCORMICK, E.
14 Akers Lane, Eccleston St.
Helens, Lancs WA10 4QL

MOXON, G
9 Savery Street
Southcoates Lane
Hull HU9 3BG

ORTON J
Occupation Road, Sibson
Nuneaton CV13 6LD

ROUNCE J.N , NDB
4 Scarborough Road
Great Walsingham
NR22 6AB

SALTER T.A , MBE
44 Edward Road, Clevedon
North Somerset BS21 7DT

SYMES, C.J
189 Marlow Bottom Road
Marlow SL7 3PL

TAYLOR, A.J
The Old Pyke Cottage
Hethelpit Cross, Staunton
GL19 3QJ

VICKERY, R.G.L
Ponderosa, Verwood Road
Three Legged Cross
Wimborne BH21 6RN

WILLIAMS, M
Tincurry, Cahir,
Co Tipperary, Eire

YOUNG, M
Mileaway, Carnreagh
Hillsborough,
Northern Island BT26 6LJ

BEE IMPROVEMENT & BEE BREEDERS' ASSOCIATION

www.bibba.com

SECRETARY
Pam Hunter
Burnthouse,
Burnthouse Lane,
Cowfold, Horsham,
West Sussex, RH13 8DH.
01403 864007
pamhunter@burnthouse.org.uk

BIBBA is an organisation devoted to encouraging beekeepers to breed native bees. The bee more suited to our environmental circumstances than other sub species. BIBBA's aims are publicised through books, workshops, lectures and conferences.

BIBBA also co-operates with worldwide Beekeeping and breeding groups interested in conserving and improving their own native bees.

MEMBERSHIP SECRETARY
David Allen
75 Newhall Road,
Doncaster. DN3 1QQ
01302 88581350
membership@bibba.com

Breeding techniques advocated include:

- Assessment of colonies by observation, recording certain criteria on standard record cards.
- Determination and purity of sub species by measurement of morphometric characters and mitrochondial DNA.
- Use of mini nucs for the mating of queens economically

SALES SECRETARY
John Hendrie
26 Coldharbour Lane
Hildenborough
Tonbridge
Kent
TN11 9JT
sales@bibba.com

BIBBA Publications include:

- The Honeybees of the British Isles by Beowulf Cooper
- Breeding Techniques and Selection for Breeding of the Honeybee by Prof. F. Ruttner
- The Dark European Honey Bee by Prof. F. Ruttner, Rev. Eric Milner and John Dews
- Breeding Better Bees using Simple Modern Methods by John E. Dews and Rev.Eric Milner
- Better Beginnings for Beekeepers by Adrian Waring - second edition.

BIBBA encourages the formation of Bee Breeding Groups, and the sharing of knowledge between groups by the provision of genetic material.
Look out for Queen Rearing events in the bee press and on www.bibba.com.

THE C.B. DENNIS BRITISH BEEKEEPERS' RESEARCH TRUST

REGISTERED CHARITY NO. 328685

Aims

This Charitable Trust was established in 1990 through the generosity of Mr. C.B. Dennis. It aims to use the interest from the capital investment to support British research projects that are likely to benefit beekeeping in the relatively short term, giving some priority to work on bee diseases.

Awards

The Trust is an independent body making awards to institutions or individuals on the basis of scientific merit of submitted proposals and perceived benefit to British beekeeping. Since the foundation of the Trust more than thirty awards in diverse areas of bee research have been made. Particular encouragement is given to young scientists through travel bursaries to enable students or researchers at the start of their careers to attend national or international meetings to present their work. A three year studentship supervised by Dr Dave Goulson at the University of Stirling has now been completed. This examined the population structure of rare and declining bumble bee species with a view to answering some key questions about their conservation. Applications for further studentships are invited.

Donations

The Trust is pleased to acknowledge the loyal support it already receives from several local beekeeping associations and many individuals. All donations, however small, will be added to the invested capital and bee research in Britain will benefit from the income in perpetuity. Supporting the Trust will ensure that sufficient income is generated to initiate the research that beekeepers would like to see undertaken.

All donations, correspondence and requests for grant application forms should be sent to the secretary

HON. SECRETARY, Ms B.V.Ball
104 Lower Luton Road
Wheathampstead
St. Albans
Herts AL4 8HH

PLEASE THINK ABOUT THIS AND HELP IF YOU CAN

All donations and correspondence should be sent to the secretary

THE CENTRAL ASSOCIATION OF BEEKEEPERS

www.cabk.org.uk

SECRETARY, Pat Allen
8 Frank's Cottages
St Mary's Lane
Upminster, RM14 3NU

PRESIDENT, Prof. R.S. Pickard
Consumer's Association
2 Marylebone Rd
London, NW1 4DF

TREASURER, John Hendrie
26 Coldharbour Lane
Hildeborough
Tonbridge, TN11 9JT

PROGRAMME SECRETARY
Pam Hunter
Burnthouse
Burnthouse Lane
Cowfold, Horsham
RH13 8DH

EDITOR, Pat Allen
8, Frank's Cottages
St. Mary's Lane
Upminster, RM14 3NU

SALES AND DISTRIBUTION,
Margaret Thomas
The Battinbuin Bothy
Battinbuin, Strathtay,
Pitlochy, PH9 0LP

The Central Association of Beekeepers in its present form dates from the time of the reorganisation of the British Beekeepers' Association in 1945. The BBKA was originally made up of private members only. However as County Associations were formed they applied for affiliation and were later permitted to send delegates to meetings of the Central Association, as the private members were then known. This arrangement became unsatisfactory as the voting power of the Central Association greatly outnumbered that of the County Associations and so in 1945 a new Constitution was drawn up whereby the Council comprised Delegates from the Counties and Specialist Member Associations. The private members then formed themselves into a Specialist Member Association with the designation 'The Central Association of the British Beekeepers' Association'; this was later shortened to its present style.

The Association was able to devote itself to its own particular aims, to promote interest in current thought and findings about beekeeping and aspects of entomology related to honey-bees and other social insects. Lectures given by scientists and other specialists are arranged, printed and circulated to members, as has been done since 1879.

An annual Spring Conference is held in London and an Autumn Conference in the Midlands. In addition, a lecture is presented at the Annual General Meeting and at the Social Evening held during the National Honey Show. The subscription is £10.00 per annum, £12.00 for dual membership (one copy only of publications).

COUNTY BEEKEEPING MAGAZINES AND NEWSLETTERS

AVON, Ms Julie Young
1 Church Cottages
Abson Road, Abson Wick
Bristol, BS30 5TT
0117 937 2156
julieyoung@btinternet.com

BEDFORDSHIRE, Sue Lang
154a Lower Shelton Road, Upper Shelton
Marston Moretaine
Beds, MK43 0LS
01234 764180
07879 848550
bedfordshirehoney@hotmail.co.uk

BERKSHIRE, Ron Crocker
25 Ship Lake Bottom
Peppard Common
Oxon RG9 5HH

CAMBRIDGESHIRE, Mr. Chris Evans
7 The Furlongs,
Needingworth,
St. Ives,
Cambs. PE27 4TX

CHESHIRE, Pete Sutcliffe
2 Hatfield Court
Holmes Chapel,
Cheshire, CW4 7HP
h.p.sutcliffe@googlemail.com.

CHESTERFIELD & DISTRICT Mrs Margaret Edge
4 Cinder Hill,
Shireoaks,
Worksop, S81 8NR

CORNWALL, Gillian Searle
6 Harleigh Road, Bodmin
Cornwall PL31 1AQ

CUMBRIA, Dave Bates
Greenfield House
Low Green
Temple Sowerby
Penrith CA10 1SD

DERBYSHIRE, Mrs. M. Cowley
14 Montpelier, Quorndon
Derby DE22 5JW

DEVON, Glyn R Davies
Landscore
Eastern Rd, Ashburton
Devon TQ13 7AR
01364 652640
landscore@eclipse.co.uk

DORSET, Richard Norman
19, Broughton Crescent
Wyke Regis, Weymouth
Dorset, DT4 9AS

DURHAM, George Eames
11, Sharon Avenue,
Kelloe,
Durham DH6 4NE
07970 926250
beeseames@btinternet.com

ESSEX, Pat Allen
8 Franks Cottages
St Mary's Lane
Upminster RM14 3NU

GLOUCESTERSHIRE, Mrs A Ellis
19 Whaddon Road
Cheltenham
Gloucestershire GL52 5LZ

GUERNSEY BKA Ruth Collins
Colombier House
Torteval
Guernsey GY8 0NF

GWENT, Keith Allen
Pen-y-Lan Cottage,
Far Hill, Trellech,
Monmouth, NP25 4PP
kh.allen@virgin.net

HAMPSHIRE, Dr Helen Harley
Communications Manager
Programme Management Unit (PMU)
University of Southampton
Bassett House
Chetwynd Road
Southampton SO16 3TU
Tel: 023 8059 2804

HEREFORDSHIRE, Mr. Len Dixon
The Square,
Titley Kington, HR5 3RG
beeline2ljd@yahoo.co.uk

BEE MAGS

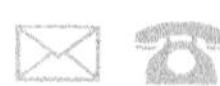

HERTFORDSHIRE
Paul Cooper
01279 771231
HUNTINGDON
Wilma Vaughan
Lauriston Copse
Warboys, Huntingdon
Cambs PE28 2US
KENDAL & SOUTH WESTMORLAND
Roger Blocksidge
20 Fowl Ing Lane
Kendal
Cumbria
LA9 6HB
tinky_winky@hotmail.com
KENT,John Hendrie
26, Coldharbour Lane,Hildenborough,
Tonbridge Kent
TN11 9JT
LEEDS BEEKEEPER
Editor Bill Cadmore,
104 Hall Lane
Horsforth, Leeds
LS18 5JG
0113 2160482
leeds.
bill.cadmore@ntlworld.com
LEICS. & RUTLAND
Editor, T. Strachan
54 Burgess Rd.
Coalville,
Leicestershire LE67 3PX
terry@trs-net.co.uk

LINCOLNSHIRE, P. Raines
Grange Cottage
21 Humberston Av.
Humberstone
Grimsby DN36 4SL
LONDON, Steve Bembow
156 D evon Mansions
Tooley Street
London SE1 2NR
MEDWAY, Rob Smith
robert_787@hotmail.com
MOLE A. CLUB,
Dennis Cutler
70 Hurst Road
East Molesey
Surrey KT8 9AG
NEWCASTLE, George Batey
Rift Farm Cottage
Wylam NE41 8BL
NORFOLK, Michael Lancefield
Candlemas House
Fakenham Road
Stanhoe
King's Lynn PE31 8PX
lancefield@aol.com
NOTHAMPTONSHIRE
Roger G Virgo
5 Surfleet Close, Corby
Northamptonshire
NN18 9BG
amellifera@aol.com
NOTTINGHAMSH,
Stuart Ching
122 Marshall Hill Drive
Porchester
Notts NG3 6HW

SOMERSET, Richard Bache
The Annex,
Moorview Farm
Midelney Road
Drayton, Near langport
Somerset, TA10 0LW
newsletter@somersetbeekeepers.org.uk
SUFFOLK, Tony Molesworth
Kizimbani, Bildeston Road, Combs. IP14 2JZ
tony.molesworth@essex.businesslink.co.uk
WARWICKSHIRE, Rob Jones
124 Ashfurlong Road
Sutton Coldfield
B75 6EW
0121 378 0562
wbeditor@warwickshire-beekeepers.org.uk
WILTSHIRE,
Ronald A Hoskins,
10 Larksfield
Covingham Park
Swindon SN3 5AD
WORCESTER,
Mrs U Brandwood
10 Monnow Close
Droitwich
Worcester WR9 8T
Ursula@brandwoodu.freeserve.co.uk
YORKSHIRE
Newsletter Editor,
Bill Cadmore,
104 Hall Lane, Horsforth
Leeds LS18 5JG
0113 216 0482
bill.cadmore@ntlworld.com

CONBA UK, COUNCIL OF THE NATIONAL BEEKEEPING ASSOCIATIONS IN THE UNITED KINGDOM

CONBA was established in 1978 to promote the aims and objectives of the national beekeeping associations of England, Scotland, Ulster and Wales. Its purpose is to represent the interests of beekeepers' with local, national and international authorities. A representative delegate from each of the member country associations occupies the chair for a period of two years, on a rotational basis.

The council meets twice per year, normally at Stoneleigh and at the National Honey Show in London, with the remaining meeting by rotation in the member association's country. Council business consists of any matters of common interest to all its members.

CONBA provides representation of its membership at the European Union (EU) through two specific committees, COPA and COGECA (COPA – Comite des Organisations Professionelles Agricoles de la CEE); (COGECA Comite de la Cooperation Agricole de la CEE); and the Honey Working Party (HWP).

The Honey Working Party meetings are held at Brussels. This committee liases with the European Commission in relation to apicultural matters concerning the member states of the European Union (EU). These matters are subsequently presented to the European Parliament for its consideration, implementation or revision or rejection. The subsequent approval of such matters results in establishing legislation, government support and possible EC funding relating to the practice of apicultural production in the UK through its membership of the EU.

INCORPORATING THE BEEKEEPING ORGANISATIONS OF:
England, Channel Islands Isle of Man, Scotland, Ulster, Wales

SECRETARY
Terry Gibson. MSc.
17 Ffolkes Drive,
Gaywood,
King's Lynn, Norfolk.
PE30 3BX.
01553 674051
bee-aware@gmx.com

CHAIRMAN, Dinah Sweet
Graigfawr Lodge,
Caerphilly CF83 1NF
sweetd@cardiff.ac.uk

VICE-CHAIRMAN, Mervyn Eddie
eddie_mervyn@yahoo.co.uk

HON. TREASURER, Martin Tovey
11, Coach Road,
Carnforth, Lancashire,
LA5 9PP.
martintovey@hotmail.co.uk

COUNCILLORS REPRESENTING THE MEMBER ASSOCIATIONS

British Beekeepers' Association, (England, Channel Islands and the Isle of Man) Chris Deaves and Pamela Hunter.

Bee Farmers, David Bancalari and John Howat

Scottish Beekeepers' Association, Ian Craig and Phil McAnespie

Ulster Beekeepers' Association, Mervyn Eddie and David Wright

FIBKA. Michael Gleeson

Welsh Beekeepers' Association, Wally Shaw and Dinah Sweet.

DEVON APICULTURAL RESEARCH GROUP

DARG is an independent group of experienced enthusiastic beekeepers whose primary aim is to collect and analyse data on matters of topical interest which may assist their apicultural education and promote the advancement of beekeeping. At their monthly meetings, DARG members discuss various topics in open forum, during which they exchange ideas and information from their personal beekeeping knowledge and experience. They also undertake suitable research projects which further the Group's aims.

TOPICS CURRENTLY BEING UNDERTAKEN

- Use of Shook Colonies and Comb Change in the control of brood diseases.
- Methods of Integrated Pest Management for the control of varroa.
- Honeybee genetics with particular reference to the selection of breeder queens.
- A survey of Useful bee plants, shrubs and trees in the South West.

PUBLICATIONS AVAILABLE

- **The Beeway Code.** A common sense guide for beginners to help avoid problems with neighbours and produce a safe and peaceful apiary.
- **Seasonal Management.** A useful aid to planning your work effectively
- **Living with Varroa jacobsoni.** A best selling title and an invaluable weapon in winning the war against the mite - updated in 1999
- **Queen Rearing.** Providing detailed help in rearing new queens in order to promote vigorous colonies.
- **Selection of Apiary Sites** full of tips for choosing the right sites for your bees.

CHAIRMAN, Richard Ball
Stoneyford Farmhouse
Colaton Raleigh
Sidmouth
Devon EX10 0HZ
HON SECRETARY, Kingsley Law
Halwell Farm, Denbury
Newton Abbot, TQ12 6ED
0180 381 2285

PUBLICATIONS OFFICER, David Loo
25 Woodlands
Newton-St-Cyres, Exeter
Devon EX5 5BP
0139 285 1472

TREASURER, Bob Ogden
Pennymoor Cottage
Pennymoor
Tiverton
Deven EX16 8LJ
01363 866687

All titles cost £2.50 per copy (post free) from the Publications Officer (tel. 01392 851472). Discounts are available for BBKA affiliated Associations **Please contact the Publications Officer for details**

THE EASTERN APICULTURAL SOCIETY OF NORTH AMERICA

www.easternapiculture.org

Kathy Summers, 623 West Liberty Street, Medina Ohio 44256
Kathy@BeeCulture.com

The Eastern Apicultural Society of North America www.easternapiculture.org) holds its annual Short Course and Conference the first full week of August, 2009, at Holiday Valley Resort and Conference Center, in Ellicotville, New York. Ellicotville is in western New York, just south of Buffalo, New York. Holiday Valley is a superb setting for this conference with first rate facilities.

We start with our intensive 3-day, 2-level Short Course, ...a starter's course, taught by our own EAS Master Beekeepers, focusing on on keeping your bees healthy and alive; and an advanced course looking at a variety of topics for experienced beekeepers. A new feature will be our anatomy class...look for that extra in the program one evening. There is plenty of hands-on bee work at our Conference, with 20 on-site colonies available, and a commercial queen breeding yard just down the road.

The theme for this year's Conference is "Toward Chemical Free Beekeeping". Speakers include Dr. Tom Rinderer from the USDA Honey Bee Research Lab at Baton Rouge, Louisiana, who developed the Russian Honey Bee, and Bob Brachman, commercial Russian Queen Breeder, Kirk Webster Kent Williams and Mike Palmer will also be there. They successfully use Russians in their operatons.

Other speakers include Dr. Tom Seeley and Dr. Nick Calderone from Cornell, Dr. Dave Tarpy from North Carolina, Dr. Jeff Pettis, USDA Research Leader and the best source of information on Colony Collapse Disorder and more.

Plus, there's Commercial beekeeper Andy Card and his family's operation right there in Ellicotville who run just over 20,000 colonies in New England and Louisiana, moving half to California to pollinate almonds. One of Andy's largest extraction facilities is here and tours show how he manages his operation to make honey and pollinate crops. And don't forget our many Vendors who have everything new in beekeeping available onsite.

Watch our web page at www.easternapiculture.org for updates and secure online registration beginning in May or so. For more information contact Kim Flottum at Kim@BeeCulture.com.

THE FEDERATION OF IRISH BEEKEEPERS' ASSOCIATIONS

http://www.irishbeekeeping.ie

Comhnascadh Cumann Beachairi na hEireann

ANNUAL SUMMER COURSE

The 2010 Beekeeping Summer Course held at the Franciscan College, Gormanston, Co Meath will take place from 26th of July to Saturday 31st July 2010. Guest Speaker will be Mr Dewey Caron from the University of Delaware, America. Dewey is Professor of Entomology & Applied Ecology at the College of Agricultural & National Resources at the University of Delaware, USA.
Full course including accommodation and meals €310. For reservation, send deposit of €40 to Summer Course Convenor: Mr Gerry Ryan, Deerpark, Dundrum, Co Tipperary (062-71274) or Email ryansfancy@gmail.com

PUBLICATIONS

- **Beekeeping in Ireland - A History** - J.K. Watson

This book gives the history of the craft from time immemorial to the present. It is well bound, hard backed and excellently presented. There are 293 pages of valuable information and 53 pictures of prominent beekeepers past and present. Price €7.00

- **Bees, Hives and Honey** - Published by F.I.B.K.A. - Edited by Eddie O'Sullivan.

This book has been compiled from writings by some of Ireland's most prominent beekeepers of the present day. It is an instruction book on beekeeping published as a millennium project and should prove a modern treatise on the craft of beekeeping and its associated products. There are over 200 pages, also many photographs and illustrations. Price €12.70 (Paperback) or €19 (Hardback)
Available from Eddie O'Sullivan, Phone: 021-4542614, Email : eosbee@indigo.ie

HON. SECRETARY
Mr. Michael G. Gleeson
Ballinakill Enfield Co. Meath
046 9541433
e-mail, mgglee@eircom.net

PRESIDENT
Mr Dennis Ryan
Mylerstown, Clonmel, Co Tipperary, 052 25600
Email dryan266@eircom.net

VICE PRESIDENT
Mr Seamus Reddy
8 Tower View Park, Kildare,
045 521945
Email
seamusreddy@eircom.net

PRO Mr P.McCabe,
"Sherdara"
Beuaulieu Cross
Drogheda, Co. Louth
041 983 6159
philipmccabe@eircom.net

HON. EDITOR, Jim Ryan
Innisfail, Kickham Street
Thurles, Co Tipperary
0504 22228
jimbee1@eircom.net

HON. MANAGER, Mr. David Lee
Scart, Kildorry, Co. Cork
022 25595
davidleej@eircom.net

HON. TREASURER, Mrs Bridie Terry
"Ait na Greine", Coolbay
Cloyne, Midleton,Co Cork
0214652141
aitnagreine@gmail.com

EDUCATION OFFICER Dr. Brendan Coughlan
Ard na gCloch, Corcullen
Moycullen, Co. Galway
091 555211
B.OCochlain@irishbroad-band.net

LIBRARIAN Jim Ryan.
Innisfail, Kickham Sr
Thurles,co Tipperary
jimbee1@eircom.net

SUMMER COURSE CONVENER Mr Gerry Ryan
Deerpark, Dundrum,
Co Tipperary
062 71274
ryansfancy@gmail.com

HONEY SHOW SECRETARY Mr R Williams
Tincurry
Cahir
Co Tipperary, Eire
052 7442617
emwilliams@eircom.net

• **The Irish Bee Guide** - Reverend J.D. Dgges
First published in 1904, It was proclaimed as an excellent book on beekeeping. It also won a place as a notable production in the literary context. It eventually ran to sixteen editions and sold seventy-six thousand copies overall. The name was changed in the second issue to The Practical Bee Guide. Now, one hundred years later, a decision has been taken to honour this great work. What better way to do it than to re-issue the book as it was in 1904 when it first entered the literary world. The re-print is an exact replica of the original first edition. The price per copy is Hardback €30 and Softback €20
Available from Eddie O'Sullivan, Phone : 021-4542614, Email: eosbee@indigo.ie

• **An Beachaire** - The Irish Beekeeper
the monthly organ of FIBKA, subscription £20.00 Stg post free from The Manager. Readership of the Journal in Northern Ireland carries third party insurance public liability cover up to €6.500,000 on any one claim and product liability cover up to €6.500,000 on any one claim, on payment of £5.00 Stg extra.

LIBRARY

The library is owned and controlled by FIBKA. It contains very many valuable books ancient and modern, available to members for return postage only. The Librarian is Jim Ryan, Innisfail, Kickham Street, Thurles, Co Tipperary.
Email: jimbee1@eircom.net

CORRESPONDENCE COURSES

The Examination Board has sponsored correspondence courses for candidates preparing for the Intermediate and Senior (Bee Masters) Examinations. Applications to John Cunningham, Ballygarron, Kilmeaden, Co Waterford, Tel No 051-399897/086-8399108 Email: john3cunningham@hotmail.com

EXAMINATIONS

The Board conducts five grades of examinations at the annual Summer Course at Gormanston College: Preliminary, Intermediate, Senior, Lecturer and Honey Judge. Preliminary and Intermediate Examinations are also held at Provincial centres in May each year.

EDUCATION

The Federation Examinations are recognised as Third Level Examinations by the National Council for Educational Awards (NCEA), thus candidates who pass the Senior Examination may apply to the NCEA for a National Certificate in Science (Apiculture) and candidates who have passed the Lectureship

Examination and who have at least two years' experience as Lecturers and who have also gained a sufficient standing in the beekeeping community may apply to the NCEA for a Diploma in Science (Apiculture), these awards are conferred by the Cork Institute of Technology (CIT) under a programme of Experiential Learning, for the Diploma a comprehensive Portfolio must be submitted to CIT, successful candidates are entitled to use the qualification NatDipSc (Apic).

Courses for beginners are run by Affiliated Associations and the FIBKA holds an Annual Summer Course in Gormanston College in July. The course caters for the three grades of students: beginners, intermediate, and senior and covers the theory and practice of modern apiculture. Examinations are held in these grades and also at Honey Judge and Lecturer level. Further information on the Examinations may be obtained from the Education Officer, Dr Brendan Coughlan, Chemistry Department, National University of Ireland, Galway (e-mail : B.OCochlain@irishbroadband.net)

NATIONAL HONEY SHOW

This is held at Gormanston College in conjunction with the annual Beekeeping Course. The Schedule contains 32 Open Classes and 3 Confined classes with €1,000 in prizes. Over 30 Challenge Cups and Trophies are presented for the competition.

Honey Show Secretary: Mr Redmond Williams, Tincurry, Cahir, Co Tipperary Tel No 052-7442617 e-mail: emwilliams@eircom.net

INSURANCE

The limit of indemnity of public liability policy is €6.500,000 arising from one accident or series of accidents. There is also product liability of €6.500,000 arising from any one claim. The policy extends to all registered affiliated members whose subscriptions are fully paid up on the 31st December of any one year and whose names are entered in the FIBKA register held by the Treasurer.

LIFE VICE PRESIDENTS

Mr. M.I Moynihan
41 Caseyville, Dungarvan
Co. Waterford
058 42389

Mr. P. O'Reilly
11 Our Lady's Place,
Naas Co. Kildare
045 897568

Mr. M.L. Woulfe
Railway House, Midleton
Co. Cork
021 631011

Mrs Frances Kane
Firmount, Clane,
Co Kildare,
087 2450640
or 045 893150

ASSOCIATION SECRETARIES

ASHFORD, Mr Michael Giles
55 Saunders Lane, Rathnew,
Co Wicklow
086-8369152

BANNER,Ms Aoife Nic Giolla
Blossom Lodge, Derra,
Kilkisken, Co Clare.
087 6743030

CARBERY, MrSean O'Donovan
Drominidy, Drimologue
Co Cork, 087 7715001

CARLOW, Mr. John Lennon
31 Idrone Park, Tullow Road,
Carlow 059 9141315

CO. CAVAN, Ms Christine Grey
Tullyvin, Cootehill, Co Craven
049 5553164

CO. CORK, Mr Robert McCutcheon
Clancoolemore, Bandon,
Cork. 023-41714

CO. DONEGALMr Derek Byrne
Carrick West, Laghey
Co.Donegal
074 9722340

CO. DUBLIN, Mr Liam McGarry
24 Quinns Road, Shankill,
Co Dublin.
087-2643492

CO. GALWAY,
Dr. Brendan Coughlan
Ard na gCloch, Corcullen,
Galway
091 555211

CO. KERRY, Mr Ruary Rudd
Westgate, Waterville,
Co. Kerry
066 9474251

CO. LIMERICK, Mr. Sean Flavin
Creeves Cross,
Shanagolden, Co. Limerick
069 60328

CO. LOUTH,
Ms Patricia Finlay Hanratty
Grey Acre, Kilkerley,
Dundalk, Co Louth.
042-9329153 or 087-0640413
CO. LONGFORD,
Mrs Brigit Koston
Sunnyside House
Loughgowna, Co. Cavan
043 83285
CO. MAYO Mrs. Cathy Dunne,
Cloofinish, Swinford,
Co. Mayo 094 9252543
CO. OFFALY,
Mr Cyril Page
Woodford, Loughrea,
Co Galway.
0906-749025/086-8043072
CO. WATERFORD
Mr Pat Dillane,
Coolbagh, Clashmore,
Co. Waterford
02496979
CO. WEXFORD
Mr. Padraig McKenna
Blake Cottage, Curracloe,
Co. Wexford
DUNHALLOW,
Mr Andrew Bourke,
Pallas, Lombardstown,
Mallow, Co Cork
087 2783807
DUNAMAISE,
Mr Seamus Brennan
Bondra,Colt,
Ballyroan, Co Laois
057 8731871
DUNMANWAY,
Mr. Michael I O'Sullivan
Ballyhalwick Dunmanway,
Co. Cork (023) 45257
EAST CORK, Mr C Terry
"Ait na Graine", Coolbay
Cloyne, Co. Cork
021 4652141
EAST WATERFORD
Mr. Michael Hughes
51 Woodlawn Grove
Cork St, Waterford
051 373461
FINGAL, Mr John McMullan
34 Ard na Mara Crescent
Malahide, Co. Dublin
(01) 8450193
FOYLE, P J Costello
Lr Drumaiveir, Greencastle
Co Donegal
074 9381303
GOREY, Mr Joe Nealon
Aspen Woods,
Raheenteigue, Tinahely,
Co Wicklow.
0402-38481
INNISHOWEN,
Mr Paddy McDonagh,
Milltownwn, Carndonagh
Co. Donegal 074 9374881
KILLORGLIN, Mr Mike Cronin
Upper Tullig,
Killorglin, Co Kerry
066-9769892
KILTERNAN
Ms. Mary Montaut
4 Mount Pleasant Villas
Bray, Co. Wicklow
01 2860497
MID KILKENNY,
Mr John Ryan
Kiltown, Castlecomer,
Co Kilkenny.
056-4441375
NEW ROSS,
Mr Seamus Kennedy
Churchtown, Fethard-on-Sea,
New Ross, Co. Wexford
051 397259
NORTH CORK, Mr Moss Guiry
Belview, Bruree, Co Limerick
061-397040
NORTH KILDARE, Mr Sean Byrne
53 Moorfielf Park,
Newbridge, Co. Kildare
045 432048
NORTH MONAHGAN
Mrs Joanna McGlaughlin
35 CastleLane,
Caledon,
Co. Tyrone, BT68 4UB
048 37569548
NORTH TIPPERARY,
Mr. Jim Ryan
"Innisfail" Kirkham St
Thurles, Co. Tipperary
0504 22228
ROUNDWOOD, Mrs M O'Byrne
Carrig View, Moneystown
South, Roundwood,
Wicklow 0404 45209
S. KILDARE,
Mr Mike Cummins
Garretfield, Donard,
Co Wicklow.
087-2726177
S. KILKENNY,
Mr Richard Moran
Kilbline, Bennetsbridge,
Co Kilkenny.
056-7727457
S. TIPPERARY, Mr Tom Prendergast
Ballypatrick, Clonmel,
Co Tipperary
087 9109360
S. WEST CORK,Mr John Bryan
Currarane,Kilbrittan,
Co Cork, 023 49625
S. WEXFORD,Mr James Hogan
Castlebridge,
Co Wexford,
053 9159202
SUCK VALLEY, Mr Frank Kenny
Stonepark, Roscommon
0906 626156
THE KINGDOM, Mr Jim Clerkin,
Arabella House
Ballymacelligott,Tralee
Co Kerry,
066 7137611
THE MIDLAND BEEKEEPERS
Mr Jim Donohoe
11 New Ballinderry, Mullingar,
Co Westmeath
044-9340771/086-2555729
THE ROYAL CO
Mrs Martina Keegan
Grange, Bective, Navan,
Co Meath, 046 9029216
WEST CORK
Mr Donald Hanley
Bawnard, Eyeries,
Co Cork,
027 74187

INTERNATIONAL BEE RESEARCH ASSOCIATION WEB http://www.ibra.org.uk

IBRA - International Bee Research Association promotes the value of bees by providing information on bee science and beekeeping. This charity was founded in 1949 and is supported by members from around the world. IBRA owns one of the largest international collections of bee books and journals, as well as the Eva Crane / IBRA historical collection and a photographic collection. It operates an online bookshop, publishes its own books and information leaflets, as well as scientific journals.

CORRESPONDENCE TO:
EXECUTIVE DIRECTOR,
Sarah Jones
SCIENTIFIC DIRECTOR,
Norman Carreck

16 North Road,
Cardiff,
CF10 3DY
Tel: 029 2037 2409
Fax: 056 0113 5640
Email: mail@ibra.org.uk

PUBLICATIONS

Journal of Apicultural Research

A peer reviewed scientific journal that's worldwide and world class. This quarterly publication contains the latest high quality original research from around the world, covering aspects of biology, ecology, natural history and culture of all types of bees.

Bee World

The flagship publication for IBRA members. Back after a 4 year hiatus this international journal provides a world view on bees and beekeeping. It covers all topics from bee history to the latest finding in bee science.

Journal of ApiProduct and ApiMedical Science

The latest online publication from IBRA launched in 2009. This peer reviewed journal is dedicated to publishing the latest scientific research on the therapeutic properties of hive products. For more information: www.jaas.org.uk

IBRA BOOKSHOP

The bookshop is accessible via the web site. To support our charitable status IBRA sells a wide range of publications at competitive prices as well as posters, gifts, DVD's and sundries. IBRA is also a publishing house and offers its members a reduction on IBRA products.

MEMBERSHIP

IBRA is proud of its international status and this is reflected by its members who join from all over the world. The membership package now offers more value than ever before: quarterly issues of Bee World, a discount on IBRA publications and online access to a growing back catalogue. For other benefits and the latest information please visit the web site.

Information about all IBRA publications and services can be found via our web site: www.ibra.org.uk

THE INSTITUTE OF NORTHERN IRELAND BEEKEEPERS (INIB)

www.inibeekeepers.com

Annual Conference 7th November 2009.
Hosted by Roe Valley beekeepers Association
Annual Honey Show 21st November 2009.

Objects of the Institute

The Institute is established to advance the service of apiculture and to promote and foster the education of the people of Northern Ireland and surrounding environs without distinction of age, gender, disability, sexual orientation, nationality, ethnic identity, political or religious opinion, by associating the statutory authorities, community and voluntary organisations and the inhabitants in a common effort to advance education, and in particular:

a) to raise awareness amongst the beneficiaries about bees, bee-keeping and methods of management;
b) to foster an atmosphere of mutual support among bee-keepers and to encourage the sharing of information and provision of helpful assistance amongst each other.

Affiliation

INIB is affiliated to the British Beekeepers Association.
With 14,000 members the British Beekeepers Association (BBKA) is the leading organisation representing beekeepers within the UK.
As an INIB member, affiliation gives the following benefits.

- BBKA News
- Public Liability Insurance
- Product Liability Insurance
- Bee Disease Insurance available
- Free Information Leaflets to Download
- Members Password Protected Area and Discussion Forum
- Correspondence Courses
- Examination and Assessment Programme
- Telephone Information
- Research Support
- Legal advice
- Representation and lobbying of Government, EU and official bodies.

Clogher Valley Beekeepers Association is affiliated to INIB
Email: cloghervalley@onlineni.net

Events

The Institute holds an annual conference and honey show. The Institute brings to Northern Ireland world renowned expert speakers from USA and Europe to give talks to beekeepers on the latest research and up to date beekeeping methods.

Education

Demonstrations on various topics such as mead making, preparing honey for shows are held during the year.
Courses for honey judges are available.

Honey Bees On Line Studies

As a result of our Association with Professor Jurgen Tautz of BEEgroup Biozentrum Universitaet Wuerzburg INIB is delighted to have introduced Honey Bees On Line Studies into Wallace High School, Lisburn a unique world wide project for schools to study bees on line. http://www.beegroup.de

SECRETARY
Caroline Thomson
105 Cidercourt Road
Crumlin
BT29 4RX
02894453655
bridgeconsultancy@
ni-home.co.uk

CHAIRMAN
Michael Young MBE
101 Carnreagh,
Hillsborough
BT26 6LJ
02892689724
myoungjudge@
yahoo.co.uk

Holders of the Institute of Northern Ireland Beekeepers Honey Judge Certificate

001.	MICHAEL BADGER MBE	01132 945879	BUZZ.BUZZ@NTLWORLD.COM
002.	GAIL ORR	02892 638363	GAIL.ORR@BELFASTTRUST.HSCNI.NET
003.	CECIL MCMULLAN	02892 638675	MADELINE.MCMULLAN@HOTMAIL.CO.UK
004.	HUGH MCBRIDE	02825 640872	LORRAINE.MCBRIDE@CARE4FREE.NET
005.	LORRAINE MC BRIDE	02825 640872	LORRAINE.MCBRIDE@CARE4FREE.NET
006.	BILLY DOUGLAS	02897 562926	
007.	MICHAEL YOUNG MBE	02892 689724	MYOUNGJUDGE@YAHOO.CO.UK
008.	FRANCIS CAPENER	01303 254579	FRANCIS@HONEYSHOW.FREESERVE.CO.UK
009.	MARGARET DAVIES	01202 526077	MARG@JDAVIES.FREESERVE.CO.UK
010.	IAN CRAIG	01505 322684	IAN'AT'IANCRAIG.WANADOO.CO.UK
011.	DINAH SWEET	02920 756483	
012.	HENRY J FERGUSON	01550 777132	
013.	LESLIE M WEBSTER	01466 771351	LESWEBSTER@MICROGRAM.CO.UK
014.	REDMOND WILLIAMS	003535242617	EMWILLIAMS@EIRCOM.NET
015.	TERRY ASHLEY	01270 760757	TERRY.ASHLEY@FERA.GSI.GOV.UK
016.	IVOR FLATMAN	01924 257089	IVORFLATMAN@SUPANET.COM
017.	ALAN WOODWARD	01302 868169	JANET.WOODWARD@VIRGIN.NET
018.	DENNIS ATKINSON	01995 602058	DHMATKINSON@TESCO.NET
019	LEO MCGUINNESS	028711 811043	PMCGUINNESS@GLENDERMOTT.COM
020	TOM CANNING	02838 871260	TOM.CANNING@VIRGIN.NET

USA

019.	ROBERT BREWER	RBREWER@ARCHES.UGA.EDU
020.	ANN HARMAN	AHWORKERB@AOL.COM
021.	BOB COLE	

LABORATORY OF APICULTURE & SOCIAL INSECTS (LASI)

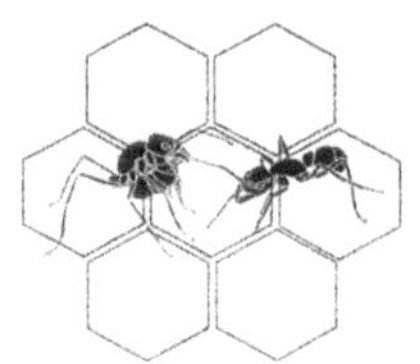

UNIVERSITY OF SUSSEX

FURTHER INFORMATION CONTACT
PDr. Francis L. W. Ratnieks, Professor of Apiculture
Laboratory of Apiculture & Social Insects (LASI)
Department of Biological & Environmental Science
University of Sussex, Falmer, Brighton BN1 9QG, UK

tel: 01273 872954 (landline), 07766270434 (mob)
F.Ratnieks@Sussex.ac.uk

LASI was founded in 1995 and is headed by Dr. Francis Ratnieks, who is the UK's only Professor of Apiculture. Professor Ratnieks received his training in honey bee biology in the USA at Cornell University and at the University of California. Also in the USA, he was a part-time commercial beekeeper with up to 180 hives used for almond pollination and comb honey production.

From 1995 to 2007 LASI was based at the University of Sheffield. In February 2008 Professor Ratnieks moved to the University of Sussex. Sussex University has provided a new laboratory that is ideal for honey bee research. There is a large adjoining apiary with an equipment shed and workshop, and the laboratory is only 100m from the main biology building. There are further apiaries on the university campus just 5 minutes walk away.

LASI is the largest university-based laboratory studying honey bees in the UK and is set up both to do research on honey bee biology and to train the next generation of honey bee scientists. Undergraduate students can do research projects on honey bee biology in their final year, and also receive lectures on honey bee biology. Graduate students can take a PhD in a particular area of honey bee biology. Postdoctoral researchers study honey bees and learn new skills to complement the training they received while doing their PhD.

LASI research focuses on both basic and applied questions in honey bee biology and beekeeping. Research areas include: how honey bees organize their colonies, how they resolve their conflicts, nestmate recognition and guarding, foraging, mating, improved beekeeping techniques, bee health and breeding, conservation of native honey bees.

LASI's mission is to be an international centre of research excellence, to train the next generation of bee researchers, and to be a resource for UK beekeepers and the public in general.

(INTER/) NATIONAL PERIODICALS

AMERICAN BEE JOURNAL
(US monthly)
Agents: Northern Bee Books
Scout Bottom Farm,
Mytholmroyd,HX7 5JS
& E.H. Thorne Ltd
Beehive Works Wragby
LN3 5LA

AUSTRALASIAN BEEKEEPER
(Monthly).
Subscriptions US$38
Sample from: Penders PMB
19 Maitland, NSW 2320
Australia

BEE CRAFT
Official monthly journal
of the British Beekeepers
Association
Subscriptions and enquiries to:
Sue Jakeman
Bee Craft Ltd
107 Church St,
Werrington
Peterborough
PE4 6QF
secretary@bee-craft.com
www.bee-craft.com
01733 771221

BEEKEEPERS QUARTERLY, THE
Companion to the
Beekeepers Annual
Subscriptions £26 p.a (but
group schemes at reduced
rates exist for BKAs)
from: Northern Bee Books
Scout Bottom Farm
Mytholmroyd, Hebden
Bridge, W. Yorkshire HX7 5JS

BERKSHIRE BEEKEEPERS ASSOCIATIONS, FEDERATION OF (FBBKA)
Newsletter Editor,
Mr R F Crocker
25 Shiplake Bottom
Peppard Common
Oxon RG9 5HH
0118 9722315
berksbees@btopenworld.com

CHESHIRE BEEKEEPER
The Newsletter of CBKA
Mr P Sutcliffe
2 Hatfield Court,
Holmes Chapel
Cheshire CW4 7HP
h.p.sutcliffe@googlemail.com

GLEANINGS IN BEE CULTURE
US monthly
From: Northern Bee Books
Scout Bottom Farm,
Mytholmroyd,HX7 5JS
& E.H. Thorne Ltd
Beehive Works Wragby
LN3 5LA

INDIAN BEE JOURNAL IN ENGLISH
1325 Sadashiv Peth, Poona
411 8030, India

INTERNATIONAL BEE RESEARCH ASSOCIATION
Journal of Apicultural Research
Journal of ApiProduct and ApiMedical Science
Bee World
enquires to:
16 North Road
Cardiff
CF10 3DY
mail@ibra.org.uk

IRISH BEEKEEPER
(Monthly) Editor: Jim Ryan
Inisfail, Kickham Street
Thurles, Co. Tipperary
jimbee1@eircom.net

THE NEW ZEALAND BEEKEEPER JOURNAL
Published 11 issues per year
for National BKA of
New Zealand
Contact: Jessica Williams
Executive Secretary
National Beekeepers
Association
PO Box 10792
Wellington 6143
New Zealand

P: + 64 4 471 6254
F: + 64 4 499 0876
Tsecretary@nba.org.nz

BEEKEEPER, THE Magazine of the Scottish BKA. Membership terms **from:** Enid Brown, Milton House, Main Street, Scotlandwell Kinross-shire KY13 9JA Sample copy to view online www.scottishbeekeepers.org.uk

SOUTH AFRICAN BEE JOURNAL Bi-monthly. P.O. Box 41 Modderfontein, 1645, RSA.

THE SPEEDY BEE Monthly US newspaper, £24 **from:** NBB, Scout Bottom Farm, Mytholmroyd Hebden Bridge HX7 5JS

GWENYNWYR CYMRU / WELSH BEEKEEPER, EDITOR, Duncan Parks Cefn Coed Graianrmon yn Ial Mold CH7 4QW 01824 780504 fax 01824 780822 e-mail, Duncan@The-Parks.com The publication of the Welsh Beekeepers Association giving news and views of beekeeping in Wales and abroad.

Golygydd/Editor: A Duncan Parks, Cefn Coed, Ffordd Graianrhyd, Llanarmon yn Ial YR WYDDGRUG CH7 4QW (01824) 780 504 e-mail, duncan@the-parks.com **Erthyglau Cymraeg:** Dewi Morris Jones, Llwynderw Bronant Aberystwyth SY23 4TG Manylion tanysgrifau/ **Subscription Details:** H. I. Morris, Golygfan Llangynin, Sancler CAERFYRDDIN SA33 4JZ 01944 290885

THE NATIONAL DIPLOMA IN BEEKEEPING

The Examinations Board for the National Diploma in Beekeeping was set up in 1954 to meet a need for a beekeeping qualification above the level of the highest certificate awarded by the British, Scottish, Welsh and Ulster Associations.

The Diploma Examination, as designed by the Board, was considered to be an appropriate qualification for a County Beekeeping Lecturer or a specialist appointment requiring a high level of academic and practical ability in beekeeping. It is the highest beekeeping qualification recognised in the British Isles and a high percentage of the past and present holders of the Diploma have given distinguished service to beekeeping education at all levels.

Although the post of County Beekeeping Lecturer has now disappeared, this has merely emphasised the need for some beekeepers to face the challenge of this examination and maintain the high level skills and knowledge needed to keep pace with the increased problems facing all beekeepers at the present time.

The Board consists of representatives from a wide range of organisations and from Government Departments and together form an impressive amalgam of expert knowledge in Beekeeping and Education. Although the National Beekeeping Associations are represented on the Board it is entirely independent of them.

Normally the highest certificate of one of the National Associations is a necessary criterion for eligibility to take the Examination for the Diploma which is held in alternate years. The Written Examination is taken in March, and the Practical, in three sections plus a viva-voce is held in June.

The Board also organises an annual Advanced Beekeeping Course covering various parts of the syllabus that are difficult to cover by independent study. Lasting

HON. SECRETARY
Norman Carreck NDB
New Hall, Small Dole,
Henfield, West Sussex.
BN5 9YJ
01273 492206
norman.carreck@
btinternet.com

CHAIRMAN, Dr David Aston NDB
38 Wressle, Selby
YO8 6ET
01757 638758

a working week, they cover the main sections of the Syllabus and represent the highest level of training available to British Beekeepers at the present time. The outside lecturers are each acknowledged experts in their particular field. In recent years the Board have been privileged to hold their course at the Fera National Bee Unit at Sand Hutton, York.

For further details regarding the Diploma write, enclosing a stamped A4 SAE to the Secretary, or visit our website: http://www.national-diploma-bees.org.uk/

Those who have gained the National Diploma in Beekeeping

Matthew Allan
Harry Allen
Harrison Ashforth
John Ashton
Dianne Askquith-Ellis
David Aston
John Atkinson
Miss E.E. Avey
Ken Basterfield
Bridget Beattie
Brig. H.T. Bell
R.W. Brooke
Norman Carreck
Rosina Clark
Charles Collins
Gerry Collins
Tom Collins
Robert Couston
John Cowan
S. J. Cox
Jim Crundwell
Beulah Cullen
Celia Davis
Ivor Davis
Alec S.C. Deans
Clive de Bruyn
A.P. Draycott
M. Feeley
Barry Fletcher
David Frimston
Oonagh Gabriel
George Gill
Reg Gove
Eric Greenwood
Pam Gregory
Anthony R.W. Griffin
Robert Hammond
Ben Harden
C.A. Harwood
Leslie Hender
Alf Hebden
Ted Hooper
Geoff Hopkinson
G. Howatson
Geoff Ingold
George Jenner
C. F. Jesson
A.C. Kessel
W.E. Large
G.W. Lumsden
Henry Luxton
A.S. McClymont
J.L. MacGregor
Ian McLean
Ian A. Maxwell
Paul Metcalf
J. Mills
Bernhard Mobus
G. N'tonga
Peter Oldrieve
Gillian Partridge
E.H. Pee
L.E. Perera
E.R. Poole
Bill Reynolds
Pat Rich
Fred Richards
E. Roberts
Arthur Rolt
Jeff Rounce
Graham Royle
J. Ryding
J.H. Savage
Donald Sims
F.G. Smith
George Smith
J.H.F. Smith
Robert Smith
Ken Stevens
J. Swarbrick
Margaret Thomas
John Walker
Adrian Waring
Brian Welch
J. Wilbraham

THE NATIONAL HONEY SHOW

www.honeyshow.co.uk
THE 2011 SHOW IS AT ST GEORGE'S COLLEGE, WEYBRIDGE, SURREY KT15 2QS
27TH – 29TH OCTOBER 2011.

This venue is excellent

Just off the M25 junction 11
Rail from Waterloo to Weybridge or Addlestone

Free car parking

The Show itself is a wonderful competitive exhibition of all the products of the bee-hive, coupled with an excellent series of lectures, workshops and a wide variety of trade and educational stands.

We recommend that you attend all three days, and suggest that you become a member of the Show – just **£10.00** per annum

For further information, please write to the Hon General Secretary, or Email: showsec@zbee.com or visit our website www.honeyshow.co.uk

HON. GENERAL SECRETARY
REV. H.F CAPENER
1 Baldric Road
Folkestone CT20 2NR

HON TREASURER
C S Mence
27 Acacia Grove
New Malden, Surrey KT3 3BJ

PUT THIS DATE IN YOUR DIARY
27TH – 29TH OCTOBER 2011

THE.NATIONAL HONEY.SHOW

www.honeyshow.co.uk
THE 2010 SHOW IS AT ST GEORGE'S COLLEGE, WEYBRIDGE
27TH - 29TH OCTOBER

ROTHAMSTED RESEARCH

www.rothamsted.bbsrc.ac.uk

ROTHAMSTED RESEARCH
Plant and Invertebrate
Ecology Division
Harpenden
Hertfordshire AL5 2JQ
Tel (01582) 763133
Fax (01582) 760981

SCIENTISTS INVOLVED IN BEE RESEARCH AT ROTHAMSTED
Dr Juliet Osborne
Alan Smith
Dr Alison Haughton
John Cussans
Dr Matthias Becher
Jennifer Swain
Dr Peter Kennedy
Andrew Martin
Dr Judith Pell
Emma Wright (PhD student)
Peter Tomkins (beekeeping support).

Rothamsted Research in Harpenden, Hertfordshire, was established in 1843 and is the world's oldest agricultural research station. There has been work on bees continuously since 1923, and despite some funding cuts and the loss of key personnel in recent years, work on bees and pollination continues as a major area of interest. We have ten scientists and students working on bee and pollination projects. A new laboratory for studying bee ecology and behaviour has been built on the Rothamsted farm, and we maintain 25 colonies of honeybees in four apiaries, with help from an experienced beekeeper who was also a previous member of staff.

We study the ecology of insect pollinators and pollen movement between plants, focussing particularly on bumblebees and honeybees. By answering fundamental questions about how bees move around at the landscape scale we hope to be able to make and test predictions about how they transport pollen around, and the consequent effects on bee-mediated plant gene flow. Our team has the overarching aims of 1) conserving and promoting bee populations and 2) protecting and promoting wild flower and crop pollination. We work primarily, but not exclusively, in arable landscapes examining pollination of plant species such as oilseed rape, white clover and borage.

EXAMINING INSECT FLIGHT PATTERNS WITH HARMONIC RADAR
Studying insect flight at a landscape scale requires sophisticated techniques. At Rothamsted we are fortunate to have the only **entomological scanning harmonic radar system** in the world for tracking individual flying

insects. We have used it to track honeybees, bumblebees and butterflies, gaining new insights into their aerial behaviour, as they search for food and fly to and from flower patches. The radar does have its limitations: it can only track insects over about 900m and that is in a relatively flat landscape with low vegetation, but it is very useful for understanding exploratory behaviour in relation to visual and olfactory cues.

HONEYBEE POPULATIONS AND PATHOLOGY

We have a new project, jointly funded by BBSRC and Syngenta (in collaboration with Warwick HRI and UFZ Leipzig) to examine the effect of multiple stressors on honeybee colony survival. Using a combination of modelling and experiments, we hope to tease apart the interactions between the effects of disease within the colony, and the effect of limited foraging sources in the landscape. We also have a PhD student studying the effects of pathogens on honeybee learning and foraging behaviour. The learning and foraging efficiency of infected and healthy colonies are being compared, and the possible impact on colony survival is then explored.

BUMBLEBEE POPULATIONS AND CONSERVATION

Bumblebees are important in agricultural systems as pollinators of crops and wild flowers, but their numbers and diversity have declined over the last 40 years, particularly in areas of intensively managed agriculture. In agricultural landscapes, the viability of bumblebee colonies depends on both the amount and spatial distribution of forage, in addition to the availability of suitable nesting sites. We use a combination of modelling, field survey, field experimentation and genetics to predict the distribution of bumblebees in arable landscapes, model their long-term viability, and to determine the impacts of change in agricultural regimes.

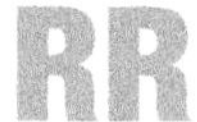

POLLINATION OF CROPS AND WILD FLOWERS AT THE LANDSCAPE SCALE

We study both the overall level of pollination in crops and wild plants in arable farmland, and also the extent of gene flow between crops or plants. We have shown that seed and fruit set in hedgerow plants can be limited by the availability of pollinators (Jacobs et al 2009). Since this affects berry production it can have a knock-on effect on the number of birds feeding on the hedges in the winter. As part of a BBSRC project (led by University of Stirling), we are examining whether wild plant pollination is influenced by the vicinity of mass-flowering crops such as oilseed rape or field beans and have also compared the pollination of these wild plants in suburban gardens versus arable farmland, showing that the plants get better pollinated in gardens and suggesting that these areas provide good resources to promote the bee populations (Cussans et al 2010).

FUNDING

Rothamsted Research receives funds for research from the BBSRC (Biotechnology and Biological Sciences Research Council of the UK), and we have also been awarded grants from Defra (Dept of Environment, Food and Rural Affairs), the European Union and commercial organisations such as Syngenta. Our research programme has also received generous support from beekeepers via the CB Dennis Fund and the BBKA and we are very grateful for this.

For more information visit
http://www.rothamsted.bbsrc.ac.uk

THE SCOTTISH BEEKEEPERS' ASSOCIATION

AIMS OF THE ASSOCIATION

- publish a monthly magazine
- maintain the Moir Library in Edinburgh
- conduct examinations in the art of beekeeping
- provide insurance and a compensation scheme for members

EDUCATION

The SBA arranges courses and awards certificates to successful candidates in the Scottish Basic Beemaster, Expert Beemaster, Honey Judge and Microscopy Examinations. It also actively promotes beekeeping by informing the public, especially the young, about bees and their benefits to the environment.

INSURANCE AND THE COMPENSATION SCHEME

All members of the SBA have insurance against Public Liability. The SBA Compensation Scheme is restricted to bee colonies located in Scotland and allocates part-replacement value for damage by vandalism, fire, theft and certain brood diseases.

LIBRARY

The SBA Moir Library in Edinburgh has one of the world's finest collection of beekeeping books. A library card is issued annually to every member who can borrow books at the cost of return postage only. Details may be obtained from the Library Convener.

MARKETS

Advice is given on all aspects of marketing honey products at appropriate times. Suggested bulk, wholesale and retail prices are notified in the magazine.

GENERAL SECRETARY
Mrs. Bronwen Wright
20 Lennox Road
Edinburgh EH5 3JW
(0131) 552 3439
e-mail, secretary@scottishbeekeepers.org.uk

HON PRESIDENT
The Rt. Hon. Earl of Mansfield D.L, J.P
Scone Palace
Perth PH2 6BE

HON. VICE PRES,
Iain F Steven
4 Craigie View
Perth
PH2 0DP
01738 621100

HON. LIBRARIAN
Mrs. Margaret M. Sharp
City Librarian, City Library
George IV Bridge, Edinburgh

HON. LEGAL ADVISER,
Taggert, Meil & Mathers
20 Bon Accord Sq,
Aberdeen
(01224) 588020

HON. AUDITOR, G. Hendry CA
20 Parkhill Crescent,
Dyce Aberdeen
(01224) 724247

PUBLICATIONS

- The Scottish Beekeeper is published monthly and sent post free as part of the annual membership fee of £25 payable to the Membership Convener.
- Introduction to Bees and Beekeeping is £6.00 plus postage and may be obtained from the Advertising and Publicity Convener.

PUBLICITY

Members can purchase the Association tie, lapel badge, car sticker etc. Details may be obtained from the Advertising and Publicity Convener.

SHOWS

Three major annual honey shows are held in Scotland. They are at the Royal Highland Show, Ingliston, Edinburgh in June, while the Scottish National Honey Show and the East of Scotland Honey Show are both held at the Dundee Flower and Food Festival in September. Shows are also held at Aberdeen, Ayr, Inverness and there are 2 shows in Fife.

Executive Committee

PRESIDENT, Alan Teale
8 Mayfield Road
Inverness IV2 4AE
01463 226411
teale@fs.com

VICE PRESIDENT, Phil McAnespie
12 Monument Road
Ayr KA7 2RL
01292 885660
membership@scottishbeekeepers.org.uk

IMM. PAST PRES, Ian Craig
30 Burnside Avenue
Brookfield
Johnstone
Renfrewshire
PA5 8UT
01505 322684
ian@iancraig.wanadoo.co.uk

GENERAL SEC Mrs. Bronwen Wright
20 Lennox Road, Edinburgh
EH5 3JW (0131) 552 3439
secretary@scottishbeekeepers.org.uk

SBA CO-ORDINATOR, Iain F. Steven
4 Craigie View, Perth PH2 0DP
01738 621100
lomand@btinternet.com

TREASURER, Mrs. Barbara Cruden
Standing Stones, Dyce
Aberdeen AB21 0HH
(01224) 770001
barbara.cruden@btinternet.com

EDITOR, SCOTTISH BEEKEEPER, Nigel Hurst
11 Munro Way,Livingston,
West Lothian,EH54 8LP
01506 439384
editorscottishbeekeepers@googlemail.com

CONVENERS OF STANDING COMMITTEES

MEMBERSHIP CONVENER
P. McAnespie
12 Monument Rd.Ayr
KA7 2RL 01292 885660
membership@
scottishbeekeepers.org.uk

INSURANCE & COMPENSATION
C. Irwin
55 Lindsaybeg Rd
Chryston, Glasgow
G69 9DW 0141 7791333

ADVERTISING & PUBLICITY
Miss E Brown
Milton House, Main Street
Scotlandwell, Kinross
KY13 9JA 01592 840582
honeybees@onetel.com

EDUCATION, Ian Craig
30 Burnside Avenue
Brookfield. Johnstone
Renfrewshire PA5 8UT
01505 322684
ian@iancraig.wanadoo.
co.uk

SHOWS, Miss E Brown
Milton House, Main Street
Scotlandwell, Kinross
KY13 9JA
01592 840582
honeybees@onetel.com

LIBRARY, Mrs Una Robertson
13 Wardie Ave
Edinburgh
EH5 2AB
una.robertson@btinternet.
com

MARKETS, John Durkacz
15 Lundin Road
Crossford
Fife KY12 8PW
01383 722186
Durkacz@hotmail.co.uk

BEE DISEASES, Gavin Ramsay
8 Parkview
Station Road
Errol
Perth PH2 7SN
01821 642385
gavinramsay@btinternet.
com

AREA REPRESENTATIVES
NORTH,
Stella Forth
Kirkland Lodge
Wardlaw Road, Kirkhill
Inverness-shire IV5 7NB
01463 831511
ibasecretary@live.co.uk

ASSISTANT NORTH
Mrs Sheila Barnard
Viewmount, Tobermory, Isle
of Mull PA75 6PG
01688 302008
tim-barnard@lineone.net

EAST, John Trout
13 Middlebank Holdings
Dunfirmline, Fife
KY11 8QN
01383 415534
dwf@fifebeekeepers.co.uk

WEST, Peter Stromberg
21 Woodside
Houston, Renfrewshire
PA6 7DD
01505 613830
pstromberg1@aol.com

ABERDEEN, Mrs. Hazel MacKenzie
Invercraig, Kingswell
Aberdeen
AB15 8PT
01224 740837
hazelmackenzie900@
btinternet/com

OFFICERS

AVA AND PROMOTION OF BEEKEEPING,
W.B. Taylor
Newbigging Cottage
Drumlithie
Stonehaven AB39 3YA
01569 740375
williet.bee@virgin.net

WEBMASTER, Alisdair Joyce
Manachie Lodge.
Dallas Dhu
Forres
IV36 0RR
01309 671288
webmaster@
scottishbeekeepers.org.uk

SPRAY LIAISON,
Leslie N Webster
Birchlea
Rothiemay, Huntly
Aberdeenshire
AB54 7LN
01466 771351
leswebster@microgram.
co.uk

S.B.A LECTURERS

*Addresses in SBA Honey Judges List

All those listed claim expenses (except G. Sharpe, Bees adviser funded by SGRPID), All speakers accompany talks with visual aids

* **MISS. E. BROWN** (General)
01592 840542
* **M BADGER** (General)
0113 2945879
* **I. CRAIG** (General)
01505 322684
A.B. FERGUSON
(General, Varroa)
Firparkneuk. Kirtlebridge
Lockerbie DG11 3LZ
01461 500322
* **C. IRWIN** (General)
0141 7791333
* **DR. F. ISLES** (Bee diseases)
01382 370 315
M.M. PETERSON
(Bee genetics)
Balhaldie House,
High street, Dunblane
FK15 0ER
01786 822093

MRS. U. A. ROBERTSON
(History of SBA, Moir Library, History of beekeeping)
13 Wardie Ave
Edinburgh EH5 2AB
0131 552 5341
G. SHARPE (SAC) (Varroa Management: My apiary management system)
Apiculture Specialist
Life Science Technology Group, SAC Auchincruive
Ayr KA6 5HW
01292 525375
* **Mrs M Thomas** (General)
Tighnabraich, Taybridge Terrace, Aberfeldy
Perthshire PH15 2BS
01887 829710

* **J. TYLER** (Strain selection and queen breeding)
22 Montgomerie Drive
Fairlie, Ayrshire
01475 568421
* **L. M. WEBSTER** (General)
01466 771351
DR G RAMSAY (Beekeeping on the Internet / Can Bees fight Varroa?)
Parkview, Station Road
Errol, Perth PH2 7SN
01821 642385
A RIACH
(Beehives through the Ages)
Woodgate, 7 Newland Ave
Bathgate
EH48 1EE
01506 653839

MEMBER ASSOCIATIONS AND THEIR SECRETARIES

ABERDEEN, Mrs Janice Kennedy
13 Harvest Hill, Westhill
Aberdeen AB32 6PU
01224 743059
AYR, Mrs L Baillie
Windyhill Cottage
Uplands Rd, Sundrum
Ayre ,KA6 5JU
01292 570659
BORDER, A.F. Mitchell
30 Parkside, Coldstream
Berwickshire TD12 4DY
01890 882683

CADDONFOOT, Mrs C Hamilton
Beechwood
Ormiston Terrace
Melrose, Roxburghshire
TD6 9SW 01896 820000
cathdech@gmail.com
CLYDE AREA, Mr George Morrison
102 Woodside Ave Bearsden
G61 2NZ
(0141) 942 9419
COWAL, Brian Madden
123a Alexandra Parade
Dunoon, PA23 8AW
01369 703317

DINGWALL Ms Sarah Smythe
14 Cromarty Drive
Strathpeffer
Ross and Cromarty
IV14 9DB
01997 420000
dingwall.beekeeping@googlemail.com

DUNBLANE & STIRLING, P. Hunt
Wildenmore, Main Street,
Gartmore FK8 3RW
01877 382594

DUNFERMLINE & WEST FIFE
J. Trout
13 Middlebank Holdings
By Dunfermline KY11 8QN
01383 415534

EAST OF SCOTLAND
Mrs. H. Kinnes
Rednock, 3 Holly Road
Broughty Ferry
Dundee DD5 2LZ
01382 477762

EAST LOTHIAN, Mrs Jo Dodds
20 Kings Avenue
Longniddry
East Lothian
EH32 0QN
01875 852916
eastlothianbeekeepers@gmail.com

EASTER ROSS
Mrs P Douglas-Menzies
Cardboll Cottage, Fearn
Ross-shire, IV20 1XP
01862 871572

EASTWOOD, Graham Matuszak
Flat1/2, 29 Herriot Street
Pollockshields
Glasgow G41 2NN
0141 418 0449
grahammatuszak@hotmail.com

EDINBURGH & MIDLOTHIAN
P Steven
Eastercowden Cottage
Dalkeith
Midlothian
EH22 2NS
07703 528801

FIFE, Janice Furness
The Dirdale, Boarhills
St. Andrews, Fife KY16 8PP
01334 880 469
jcfurness@dirdale.fsnet.co.uk

FORTINGALL, Mrs. Jo Pendleton,
Lilac Cottage
Old Bridge of Tilt
by Pitlochry
PH18 5TP
01796 481 362

GLASGOW DISTRICT,
Mr P Stromberg
21 Woodside Houston,
Renfrewshire
PA6 7DD
01505 613830

HELENSBURGH, M Thornley
Glenarn
Glenarn Road
Rhu, Helensburgh
G84 8LL
01436 820493
masthome@dsl.pipex.com

INVERNESS-SHIRE
Mrs S Forth
Kirkland Lodge
Wardlaw Road
Kirkhill, Inverness-shire
IV5 7NB
01463 831511

KELVIN VALLEY, I Ferguson
4 South Glassford Street
Milngavie
G62 6AT
0141 956 3963

KILBARCHAN AND DISTRICT
I. Craig
30 Burnside Ave
Brookfield
Johnstone PA5 8UT
01505 322684

KILMARNOCK & IRVINE
J. Campbell
North Kilbryde House
Stewarton
Kilmarnock KA3 3EP
01560 482489

KIRRIEMUIR,
'Disbanded'

LARGS & DIST, Kate Dahlstrom
3 Burnside Road
Largs
KA30 9BY
01475 740437
k.dahlstrom@btinternet.com

LOCHABER, P.J. Browne
The Rowan Tree, Gairlochy
Spean Bridge
Inverness-shire PH34 4EQ
01397 712898

MORAY, T Harris
Cowiemuir
Fochabers
01343 821 282

MULL, Mrs. S. Barnard
Viewmount, Tobermory
Isle of Mull PA75 6PG
01688 302008

NAIRN & DISTRICT,
Ms B McLean
Upper Flat,2 Inverernе Rd
Forres, IV36 1DZ
01309 676316

OBAN & DISTRICT,
Phil Moss
Ealachan Bhana
Clachan Seil
Oban
PA34 4TL
01852 300383
phil.moss@dsl.pipex.com

OLRIG and District, Robin Inglis
Roadside Skirza
Freswick, Wick KW1 4XX
01955 611260
gailinglis@btinternet.com
ORKNEY, Doris Fischler
84 Victoria street
Stromness
Orkney KW16 3BS
01856 850447
d@orcahotel.com
PEEBLES-SHIRE, G. Goldshaw
Amanda Clydesdale
20 Kingsmeadows Gardens
Peebles EH45 9LB
01721 720563
amanda.clydesdale@
btinternet.com
PERTHSHIRE, J. Shovlin
"Invercarse", 4 Glebe
Terrace, Perth PH2 7AG
01738 627965
SKYE & LOCHALSH,M Purrett
15 Glasnakille, Egol
Isle of Skye, IV49 9BQ
01471 866 207
S. OF SCOTLAND, A Ferguson
Firparkneuk
Kirtlebridge Lockerbie
DG11 3LZ 01461 500322
fergiearchie@tiscali.co.uk
SUTHERLAND, Sue Steven
Mulberry Croft, 2 East
Newport, Berriedale
Caithness KW7 6HA
01539 751 245
WEST'N GALLOWAY, Fiona Keith
The Walled Garden
Dunragit DG9 8PH
01581 400613
WEST LINTON & DISTRICT
D. Stokes
100 Main Street, Roslin
Midlothian EH25 9LT
0131 440 3477

SBA ACTIVE HONEY JUDGES

M BADGER
Kara, 14 Thorn Lane,
Roundhay,
Leeds LS8 1NN
MISS E. BROWN
Milton House, Main Street,
Scotlandwell
Kinross KY13 9JA
01592 840582
P.J. BROWNE
The Rowan Tree, Gairlochy
Spean Bridge
Inverness-shire PH34 4EQ
01397 712730
M. CANHAM
Whinhill Farm House
by Cawdor, Nairn IV12 5RF
01667 404314
I. CRAIG
30 Burnside Avenue
Brookfield, Johnstone
Renfrewshire,PA5 8UT
01505 322684
H DONOHOE
7 Grant Road
Banchory AB31 5UW
01330 823502
C. E. IRWIN
55 Lindsaybeg Road
Chryston, Glasgow
G69 9DW
0141 7791333
DR F. ISLES
"Gardenhurst",
Newbigging Broughty Ferry
Dundee DD5 3RH
01382 370315

P MATHEWS
MRS C MATHEWS
4 Annanhill
Annan, Dumfries-shire
DG12 6TN
01461 205525
MS B L MCLEAN
Upper Flat, 2 Invererne Rd,
Forres IV36 1DZ
01309 676316
W.B. TAYLOR
West Newbigging Cottage,
Glenbervie Road, Drumlithie
Stonehaven AB39 3YA
01569 740375
L.M. WEBSTER
Birchlea, Rothiemay, Huntly
Aberdeenshire AB54 5LN
01466 771351
C. WEIGHTMAN
Shilford, Stocksfield,
Northumberland NE43 4HW
01661 842082
C. WILSON
Cedarhill, Auchencloch,
Banknock, Bonnybridge
FK4 1VA
01324 840227
DR D WRIGHT
MRS B WRIGHT
20 Lennox Row
Edinburgh EH3 5JW
0131 552 3439
M. YOUNG
101 Carnreagh, Hillsborough
County Down
N. Ireland BT26 6LJ
0289 268972

Freuchie BKA disbanded

ULSTER BEEKEEPERS' ASSOCIATION

www.ubka.org

OBJECTS OF THE ASSOCIATION

The objects of the Association shall be to unite beekeepers for their mutual benefit to serve the best interests of beekeeping by all means within its power and to foster its healthy development.

For the purpose of achieving these objects the Association will:

- promote the formation of local Beekeepers' Associations
- disseminate information and advice about beekeeping
- provide examination facilities in the art of beekeeping
- encourage maintainenance and improvement of the beekeeping environment.

EDUCATION

In conjunction with the Department of Agriculture and Rural Development (DARD) the U.B.K.A. assists in organising classes for Preliminary, Intermediate and Senior Certificate Examinations in Beekeeping following the syllabus of the F.I.B.K.A.

INSURANCE

Affiliated local Assosiations and their individual members have access to the UBKA group public and product liability insurance scheme.

APIARY SITES

The ten local Associations and CAFRE's Greenmount Campus have access to apiary sites and, for some sites, access to observation houses, provided with help affiliated local Associations and CAFRE's Greenmount Campus each have an apiary site with observation houses, provided with help from Leader 2 funding,for use

SECRETARY, David McCartney
19 Delacherois Avenue
LISBURN, Co Antrim
BT27 4TR

PRESIDENT,
Mervyn Eddie
3b Old Road
Upper Ballinderry
LISBURN Co Antrim
BT28 2NJ

CHAIRMAN, David Wright
24 Quarry Road
Lisbane, Comber
NEWTOWNARDS
Co Down BT23 5NF

TREASURER, Matthew Porter.
375 Old Glenarm Road
LARNE Co Antrim
BT40 2LH

LECTURERS

Jim Fletcher
26 Coach Road, Comber
Co.Down. BT23 5QX

Ethel Irvine
2 Laragh Lee
Ballycassidy
ENNISKILLEN
BT94 2JT

Lorraine McBride
11, Ballyloughan Park
Ballymena, Co.Antrim,
BT43 5HW

Norman Walsh
43, Edentrillick Rd
Hillsborough, Co. Down
BT26 6PG

LECTURERS CONTINUED
Rev Sam Millar
41 Rectory Park
Garvagh, COLERAINE
Co Londonderry BT51 5AJ

HONEY JUDGES
Jim Fletcher
26 Coach Road, Comber
BT23 5QX
Michael Young
Mileway, Carnreagh Road
Hillsborough, Co. Down
BT26 6LJ
Norman Walsh
43 Edentrillick Rd
Hillsborough Co. Down
BT26 6NH

in demonstrating and promoting good practice to members, schools and other interested groups

HONEY SHOWS

Local Associations, Horticultural and other Societies stage honey shows throughout Northern Ireland. The Northern Ireland Honey Show hosted by the Belfast City Parks Department is held annually in September in the Botanic Gardens Belfast.

CONFERENCE

The next UBKA Annual Conference will be held on 11- 12 MARCH 2011 at CAFRE's Greenmount Campus, Antrim. Contact the U.B.K.A. Conference Manager at 028 9445 3892 and www.ubka.org for details.

SECRETARIES OF ASSOCIATIONS

BELFAST,
Alan Rea
12 Kirkliston Drive
BELFAST BT5 5NX
DROMORE AND DISTRICT,
Vanessa Drew
40 Lacken Road
Ballyroney,
Banbridge, Co.Down
BT32 5JA
EAST ANTRIM,
Fiona McGinty
1 Berkeley Deane
Greenisland
CARRICKFERGUS
Co Antrim, BT38 8FX
MID ANTRIM,
Lorraine McBride
11 Ballyloughlan Park
BALLYMENA,Co. Antrim
BT43 5HW
FERMANAGH,
Brian Richardson
agho,305 LattoneRoad,
Belcoo, ENNISKILLEN
Co. Ferman

KILLINCHY AND DISTRICT
David McCartney
19 Delacherois Ave,
Lisburn, Co. Antrim
BT27 4TR
MID ULSTER, Ernie Watterson
Flourmill Hill,
264 Coalisland Rd
DUNGANNON
Co.Tyrone BT71 6EP
RANDALSTOWN,
Caroline Thomson
105 Cidercourt Rd
Crumlin, ANTRIM,
Co. Antrim, BT29 4RX
ROE VALLEY, Billy McBride
59,Seacoast Road,
Limavady
Co. Londonderry
BT49 9DW
ROSTREVOR AND
WARRENPOINT
Cécile Maugy
5 Killowen Old Road
Rostrevor
BT34 3AD
County Down

CYMDEITHAS GWENYNWYR CYMRU WELSH BEEKEEPERS' ASSOCIATION

AMCANION Y GYMDEITHAS / AIMS OF THE ASSOCIATION

- Promote and develop beekeeping in Wales
- Conduct examinations in beekeeping
- Liaise with organisations and bodies for the benefit of beekeeping in Wales

AELODAETH UNIGOL / INDIVIDUAL MEMBERSHIP

Individual membership of the WBKA is provided for persons who do not live within the areas of branch associations, and wish to support the association. Information relating to benefits and facilities provided for individual members is available from the Individual Membership Secretary.

ARHOLIADAU / EXAMINATIONS

The Examinations Board conducts six grades of examinations: Junior, Primary, Intermediate, Practical, Honey Show Judges, Senior. Information is available from the Examination Board Secretary.

Candidates following the Duke of Edinburgh Award Scheme may receive information regarding the inclusion of beekeeping as a course submission from the Examinations Secretary.

CYNHADLEDD/ CONVENTION

At the Royal Welsh Agricultural Society's Showground, Llanelwedd. This event is normally held during Late March/ Early April. Information relating to this event is available from the convention secretary.

YSWIRIANT / INSURANCE

All individual and fully paid up members of beekeeping associations affiliated to WBKA are covered against 'Public and Product' liability claims. All affiliated associations are covered against public liability during conventions officially organised by the association.

YSGRIFENNYDD / SECRETARY
Lynfa Davies
Godre'r Coed
Devils Bridge
Aberystwyth SY23 4QY
secretary@wbka.com

LLYWYDD/PRESIDENT
Dinah Sweet,
Graig Fawr Lodge
Caerphilly
CF83 1NF
president@wbka.com

CADEIRYDD/CHAIR
Valerie Forsyth
Bwlch y Rhyd
Nanternis
New Quay
SA45 9RS
chair@wbka.com

IS-GADAIRYDD/ VICE CHAIR
Tom Pegg
depchair@wbka.com

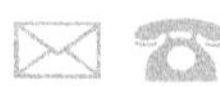

TRYSORYDD/TREASURER
Jane Jamison
Riverside House
Spring Gardens
St Dogmaels, Cardigan
SA43 3AX
treasurer@wbka.com

GWEFEISTR/WEBMASTER AND GOLYGYDD/EDITOR
Brian and Cherry Clark
editor@wbka.com

IS-OLYGYDD (ERTHYGLAU CYMRAEG)/SUB EDITOR
Dewi Morris Jones
Llwynderw, Bronant
Aberystwyth SY23 4TG
(01974 251264)

ARHOLIADAU/EXAMINATIONS
Dinah Sweet
Graig Fawr Lodge
Caerphilly
CF83 1NF
president@wbka.com

The WBKA Individual Membership benefits include cover under the BDI Scheme against the loss, due to foul brood diseases, of a minimum number of stocks (determined by BDI). Affiliated Associations provide this cover for their members.

LLYFRGELL / LIBRARY

The reference sections of all county libraries in Wales have details of the names and addresses of Secretaries of Associations affiliated to WBKA.

Books on beekeeping can be borrowed from county, branch and mobile libraries. The Library, Ffordd y Bala, Dolgellau LL40 2YS, has been nominated to stock beekeeping books.

Members of associations affiliated to IBRA may borrow books/documents from its library.

GWENYNWYR CYMRU - The Welsh Beekeeper

A publication of the Welsh Beekeepers Association, giving news and views of beekeeping and related subjects. Articles and advertisements enquiries should be sent to the Editor. Articles written in Welsh should be sent to the Sub Editor. Gwenynwyr Cymru is provided free to members of Affiliated Associations and Individual Members. Information regarding subscriptions is available from the Individual Membership / Subscription Secretary.

GWASANAETH CLYWELED / AUDIO-VISUAL AIDS SERVICE

This service is available to all affiliated associations and individual members. Further information is available from the Audio-Visual Aids Secretary.

DARLITHWYR / DANGOSWYR, LECTURERS / DEMONSTRATORS

The names and addresses of lecturers and demonstrators, recommended by associations affiliated to the WBKA, are available from the General Secretary.

CYNLLUN CYSWLLT CHWYSTRELLU / SPRAY LIAISON SCHEME

Information is available from the General secretary

SIOEAU / SHOWS

Honey/beekeeping sections are included at the Royal Welsh Agricultural Show, Llanelwedd, (OS ref: SO040520) during July, and at county, town and village shows throughout Wales. Information relating to these events may be obtained from secretaries of associations in the locality of the shows.

The historic FFAIR FEL ABERCONWY is held annually in the main street of the town, (OS ref: SH278378), on 13th September. Further information is available from the secretary of Conwy Association.

RHEOLAU CYFREITHIOL / STATUTORY REGULATIONS

The administration of the statutory regulations governing all aspects of beekeeping in Wales, is the responsibility of the Wales National Assembly, Caerdydd, CF99 1NA Phone (02920) 825111 Fax: (02920) 823352 Matters concerning statutory regulations, their implications and execution, should be addressed to the Minister of Agriculture and Rural Affairs, Wales National Assembly, at the above address.

AELODAETH UNIGOL-TANYSGRIFAU/ INDIVIDUAL MEMBERSHIP SUBSCRIPTIONS
Jane Frank
61 Fir Court Ave
Churchstoke
Montgomery, Powys
SY15 6BA
01588 620711
janefrank@bluebottle.com

YSWIRIANT/INSURANCE
CONTACT TREASURER FOR INFORMATION

INSURANCE:
Rhodri Powell
146 Pandy Rd, Bedwas,
Caerphilly CF83 8EP
rhodro@hotmail.com

AUDIO VISUAL AIDS:
F. G. Eckton
Cartref
Llanafan Fawr,
Llanfair ym Muallt LD2 3LT
01591 620456

CONVENTION SECRETARY:
John Page
john-of-pontsian@tiscali.co.uk

CONVENTION TRADE STANDS SECRETARY:
Wally Shaw
Llwyn Ysgaw, Dwyran,
Llanfairpwll, Anglesey
LL61 6RH 01248 430811
waltershaw301@btinternet.com

CYMDEITHASAU TADOGOL A'U YSGRIFENYDDION / AFFILIATED ASSOCIATIONS AND SECRETARIES

ABERYSTWYTH, Ann Ovens,
Tan-y-Cae, Nr Talybont,
Ceredigion,
SY24 5OL
01970 832359
ann.ovens@btinternet.com

ANGLESEY, Peter Edwards
Erw Newydd Llanfair ME
Tynygongl Ynys Mon
LL74 8NR
01248 853879
pwedw3@hotmail.co.uk

BRECKNOCK AND RADNOR, Dr Gillian Todd, Meadow Breeze, Llanddew, Brecon
LD3 9ST
01874610902 07971314798
gbtodd@btinternet.com

BRIDGEND, Sue Verran Ty Mel,
Maesteg Rd. Bridgend
CF32 0EE
01656 729699
verran@btinternet.com

CARDIFF AND VALE, Annie Newsam
Stonecroft, Mountain Road,
Bedwas, Caerphilly, CF83 8ER
annienewsam@hotmail.co.uk

CARMARTHEN, Brian Jones
Cwmburry Honey Farm,
Ferryside, Carmarthenshire,
SA17 5TW
01267 267318
beegeejay2003@yahoo.co.uk

CONWY, Mr Peter McFadden,
Ynys Goch
Ty'n y Groes,
Conwy LL32 8UH
01492 650851
peter@honeyfair.freeserve.co.uk

EAST CARMARTHEN
John Williams, Penrhiw,
Llansadwrn, Llanwrda,
SA19 8LP,
01550 777498,
john@penrhiw.net

FLINT AND DISTRICT,
Jill and Graham Wheeler,
Mertyn Downing, Whitford
Holywell, Flintshire,
CH8 9EP.
01745 560557
mertyndowning@btinternet.com

GWENYNWYR CYMRAEG CEREDIGION W.I.Griffiths,
Llain Deg, Comins Coch,
Aberystwyth, SY23 3BG
01970 623334
wilmair@btinternet.com

LAMPETER AND DISTRICT
Mr Gordon Lumby,
Gwynfryn, Brynteg,
Llanybydder,
SA40 9UX
01570 480571
g.lumby@btopenworld.com

LLEYN AC EIFIONYDD
Amanda Bristow, Bryngwydion,
Pontllyfni, Gwynedd
LL54 5EY 01286 831328
amanda@vosltd.com

MEIRIONNYDD, Lesley Bay,
Hen Orsaf, Gellilydan,
Blaenau-ffestiniog,
LL41 4EP
01766 590488
bazurka@aol.com

MONTGOMERY, Jessica Bennett,
Plasheulwen, Llanfair Road,
Newtown, Powys,
SY16 3JY
01686 626872
jessica.bennett@virgin.net

PEMBROKESHIRE, Mr J Dudman,
Sevenoaks, The Kilns,
Llangwm, Haverfordwest,
Pembrokeshire,
SA62 4HG
01437 891892
secretarypbka@hotmail.com>

SOUTH CLWYD,
Mrs Carol Keys-Shaw, Y Beudy,
Maesmor Hall, Maerdy
Corwen LL21 0NS
01490 460592
c.keysshaw@btinternet.com

SWANSEA, Paul Lyons,
2 West Cliff, Southgate,
Swansea, SA3 2AN.
paul.lyons@bt.com

TEIFISIDE, John Page,
The Old Tannery, Pontsian,
Llandysul, SA44 4UD
01545 590515
john-of-pontsian@tiscali.
co.uk

WEST GLAMORGAN,
Mr John Beynon,
48, Whitestone Avenue,
Bishopston,
Swansea. SA3 3DA
01792 232810,
jakbeynon@btinternet.com

HEB DADOGU/NON AFFILIATED:
Mrs J Bromley
Ty Hir, Monmouth Road
Raglan, Usk. NP15 2ET
01291 690331
bromleyjan@hotmail.com

BEIRNIAID SIOE FÊL TRWYDDEDIG / WBKA QUALIFIED HONEY SHOW

TERRY E. ASHLEY
Meadow Cottage,
11 Elton Lane, Winterley
Sandbach CW11 4TN

M. J. BADGER MBE
14 Thorn Lane, Leeds
LS8 1NN

M BESSANT
Gwili Lodge, Heol
Lotwen, Rhydaman
SA18 3RP

ROBERT BREWER
PO Box 369, Hiawassee,
Georgia, USA

TOM CANNING
151 Portadown Road,
Armagh, Co Armagh
BT61 9HL

LES CHIRNSIDE
Bryn-y-Pant Cottage,
Upper Llanover,
Abergavenny NP7 9ES

CARYS EDWARDS
Ty Cerrig, Ganllwyd,
Dolgellau LL40 2TN

IFOR C. EDWARDS
Lleifior, Pontrhydygroes,
Ystrad Meurig SY25 6DN

D.H. FERGUSON-THOMAS
Erwlon, Llanwrda
SA19 8HD

STEVEN GUEST
Bridge House, Hind
Heath Road, Sandbach,
CW11 3LY

HUGH MCBRIDE
11 Ballyloughan Park
Antrim BT43 5HW

LORRAINE MCBRIDE
11 Ballyloughan Park
Antrim BT43 5HW

CECIL MCMULLAN
33 Glebe Road,
Hillsborough, County
Down

LEO MCGUINESS
89 Dunlade Road, Grey
Steel BT47 4QL

GAIL ORR
64 Ballycrone Road,
Hillsborough BT26 6NH
Dinah Sweet
Graig Fawr Lodge,
Caerphilly, CF83 1NF

REDMOND WILLIAMS
Tincurry, Cahir, Co
Tipperary Eire

MICHAEL YOUNG MBE
Mileaway, Carnreagh,
Hillsborough BT26 6LJ

NATIONAL BEE UNIT, THE FOOD AND ENVIRONMENT RESEARCH AGENCY

www.nationalbeeunit.com

National Bee Unit
The Food and Environment Research Agency
Sand Hutton, York, YO41 1LZ, UK

Tel.No: 01904 462510
Fax.No: 01904 462240
E-Mail: nbu@fera.gsi.gov.uk
Website: www.nationalbeeunit.com
www.fera.defra.gov.uk
Policy : www.defra.gov.uk

NATIONAL BEE UNIT TECHNICAL STAFF, HEAD OF UNIT
Mike Brown

HOME BASED STAFF:

NATIONAL BEE INSPECTOR
Andy Wattam
01522 789726
07775 027524

NATIONAL BEE UNIT IS NOW UNDER THE FOOD AND ENVIRONMENT RESEARCH AGENCY (FERA)

NATIONAL BEE UNIT

The National Bee Unit (NBU) is part of the executive agency of the Department for Environment, Food and Rural Affairs (Defra), and is located based just outside York. The Unit is an element of FERA's Plant Health Group (PHG) and its work covers all aspects of bee health and husbandry in England and Wales, on behalf of Defra in England and for the Welsh Assembly Government DEPC in Wales (Department for Environment, Planning and the Countryside). The work of the unit includes disease and pest diagnosis, research into bee health matters, development of contingency plans for emerging threats, import risk analysis, related extension work and consultancy services to both government and industry.

BEE HEALTH INSPECTION SERVICE

The Integrated Bee Health Programme is run by the NBU on behalf of core policy customers. The NBU has a long track record in bee husbandry and bee disease control (since 1946) and has been directly responsible for the bee inspection services in England and Wales since 1994.

The NBU consists of a home-based inspectorate team, and the laboratory diagnostic and research team based at FERA, York. In addition colleagues across FERA contribute to the programme and research projects.

The Bee Health Inspectorate

The inspectorate team consists of approximately 45 home-based members of staff. It is headed by the

National Bee Inspector (NBI, whose role it is to run the statutory disease control and training programmes. The NBI has management responsibility for eight home-based Regional Bee Inspectors (RBIs), one heading each of the seven regions in England and one covering Wales. The RBI in turn manages a number of experienced Seasonal Bee Inspectors (SBIs). The RBIs and SBIs in England organise inspections under EU and UK legislation, submit suspect samples for diagnosis, treat colonies for foul brood and train beekeepers in bee husbandry for better disease control and greater self-sufficiency. In addition the bee inspectors also collect honey samples for residue analysis under the Statutory Honey collection agreement with Defra Veterinary Medicines Directorate (VMD). With Aethina tumida (small hive beetle (SHB)) and Tropilaelaps spp. now being notifiable under UK and EU law inspectors also undertake surveillance for these exotics in "at risk apiaries" close to ports of entry for example.

BEE DISEASE DIAGNOSTIC TEAM

The NBU's diagnostic team provides a rapid, modern diagnostic service for both the inspection service and beekeepers. The NBU laboratory is Good Laboratory Practice (GLP) compliant, a quality accreditation scheme administered by the Department of Health. All diagnostic tests are conducted according to the OIE (Office International des Epizooties) Manual of Standard Diagnostic Tests and Vaccines. The OIE is the world organisation for animal health and produce internationally recognised disease diagnosis guidelines (http//www.oie.int.) Across FERA diagnostic support is provided from teams of microbiologists acarologists, insect virologists and molecular specialists in the FERA Molecular Technology Unit (MTU).

BEES AND THE LAW

The Bees Act 1980 UK empowers Agriculture Ministers to make Orders to control pests and diseases affecting bees, and provides powers of entry for authorised persons. Under the Bees Act, The Bee Diseases and Pests Control Order 2006 for England and Wales, (there

REGIONAL BEE INSPECTORS

Andy Wattam
(Northern Region)
01522 789726
07775 027524
Mr D Sutton (Western Region)
01885 483136
07813 510676
Nigel Semmence
(Southern Region)
01264 338694
07776493649
Mr A Byham (South East Region)
01306 611016
07890 831327
Mr A Vevers (South West Region)
01364 653325
07977 336574
Keith Morgan (Eastern Region)
01485 520838
07919 004215
Mr I Flatman
(N'th Eastern Region)
01924 257089
Francis Gellatly (Wales)
01558 650663
07775 119480

FOR DETAILS OF SEASONAL BEE INSPECTORS DETAILS CONTACT THE RELEVANT RBI OR CHECK BEEBASE

LABORATORY BASED STAFF
Research Co-ordinator
Giles Budge

Laboratory & Apiary Manager
Selwyn Wilkins

LABORATORY TECHNICAL STAFF
Ben Jones

ADMINISTRATIVE OFFICERS
Commercial and Diagnostic Services Manager -
Selwyn Wilkins

Laboratory Diagnosis & Research - Benjamin Jones

Administrative Programme support -
Kate Parker & Jenna Cook

is similar legislation for Scotland and Northern Ireland) designates American foulbrood (AFB), European foulbrood (EFB), A. tumida (SHB) and Tropilaelaps mites (all species) as notifiable pests and defines the action which may be taken in the event of outbreaks.

At the European level, the Directive on animal health requirements for trade in bees is called the Balai Directive (92/65/EEC) implemented in the UK under the Animal and Animal Products (Import and Export) Regulations. It lists American foul brood (AFB), the small hive beetle (A. tumida) and Tropilaelaps mites as notifiable pests and diseases throughout the EU (at the time of writing time neither the small hive beetle nor Tropilaelaps have been confirmed in Europe).

THE IMPORTATION OF BEES

It is legal to import Queen bees from third countries, the rules governing this are set out in Commission Decision 2003/881/EC, as amended by Commission Decision 2005/60/EC. The list of countries is currently restricted to, Argentina, Australia, Hawaii and New Zealand.

It is legal to import bees freely from the EU (including queens, packages and colonies). Under the Balai directive consignments of bees moved between Member States must be accompanied by an original health certificate confirming freedom from notifiable pests and diseases.

For full details on the importation of bees from within the EU or from Third countries please either consult the Defra website (http://www.defra.gov.uk/hort/Bees/index.htm) or contact the NBU.

AMERICAN AND EUROPEAN FOUL BROOD

Foul brood-infected apiaries are placed under standstill notice, supervised by the bee inspector, until the disease is cleared from the apiary and the honey from antibiotic-treated colonies is safe to harvest. We always aim to minimise the impact of this as far as possible, in co-operation with the beekeeper.

VARROA

As part of the NBU's routine field screening programme the first known case of resistant varroa mites in the UK was discovered in apiaries in Devon in August 2001. The NBU undertook a resistance-monitoring programme throughout England and Wales. Varroa resistant mites are now widespread in England and Wales. To see the current status of the resistance of varroa mites to pyrethroids and the latest advice on treatments please visit the NBU website (http://beebase.FERA.gov.uk/).

ADULT BEE DISEASES

The NBU also look for adult bee diseases and parasites such as Nosema species (*Nosema apis* and *osema*. ceranae, amoeba (*Malpighamoeba mellificae*) and tracheal mites (*Acarine* or *Acarapis woodi*) from samples submitted by beekeepers. As these diseases are non-statutory this service is chargeable. For the current cost please contact the NBU. Bees that have been imported from designated Third countries are also checked for disease and are also screened for exotic pests potentially harmful to UK beekeeping.

EXOTICS

Beekeepers must make themselves aware of the potential threats to beekeeping in the UK. The field inspection team monitors for potential exotics, the SHB and Tropilaelaps spp. The laboratory team also routinely screen import samples and suspect samples submitted for identification by both beekeepers and the field team.

PESTICIDE MONITORING

The Wildlife Incident Investigation Scheme (WIIS) is a unique Defra scheme for monitoring the effects of pesticides on wildlife, including honey bees, and is used as a model by other countries. Samples of bees from a suspected spray poisoning incident are sent to the NBU are screened for disease prior to residue analysis by the Wildlife Incident Unit. Reports from incidents are used by the independent Environmental Panel (which reports to the Advisory Committee on Pesticides) to identify and solve any problems with the use of misuse of agrochemicals, wherever possible.

RESEARCH & DEVELOPMENT

A programme of research and development within the group underpins the Unit's work. They also have long-established links with many European and world wide research centres, beekeeping specialists and beekeepers to ensure we keep up to date with current beekeeping trends and research. Some of the most recent projects have included the development of rapid diagnostics techniques for foulbrood and viruses. Lateral flow diagnostic kits (the development of which was funded by Vita Europe Ltd) are now used routinely in the UK for the field diagnosis of AFB and EFB. There has also been the development and introduction of the Shook Swarm treatment method for EFB, which the NBU has been investigating for the past several years. We are currently working on a 'one-stop shop' for bee disease diagnosis using molecular biology techniques. The primary aim of our R & D is to provide up-to-date technical support to beekeepers and to our Bee Health Inspection Service. Also the NBU has three PhD students studying various topics including the discrimination of AFB bacteria, the taxonomy of UK honey bee viruses and the characterisation and distribution of bee diseases and parasites in Thailand. For an update on R&D work at the unit see the NBU website.

The main areas of R&D are foul brood, Varroa, exotics, viruses and the impact of agriculture on bees.

RISK ASSESSMENT

The National Bee Unit manages 150 honeybee colonies and has much experience in assessing the effects and efficacy of veterinary bee medicines (e.g., varroacides) and pesticides in both field and laboratory tests. Our Good Laboratory Practice (GLP) accreditation allows us to undertake a wide range of routine and specially designed laboratory, semi-field and field studies on honeybees and bumblebees for regulatory authorities and industry worldwide.

EXTENSION

The NBU helps train beekeepers in several ways: local courses and advisory visits run by the inspectors, and national courses held at the York laboratory. Over the past seven years the NBU has hosted National Diploma in Beekeeping residential courses and has also been host to visiting overseas workers and researchers. NBU York based staff also provide training to beekeepers at local and regional beekeeper meetings.

THE BEE HEALTH ADVISORY PANEL

This FERA panel includes representatives from the BBKA, WBKA, BFA, CONBA, and BDI. It also has independent members from the bee industry. Formed in 1999, the panel monitors the FERA National Bee Unit performance against agreed standards, but more importantly it influences modernisation of procedures under the Bees Act to cope with changes affecting industry And helps the NBU with improving the service provided for beekeepers

BEEBASE ONLINE

BeeBase is a web-based data base acting as an Information Warehouse. Originally funded by the Defra Challenge Fund, work began on this project in 2005. The database was developed the Knowledge management group (part of FERA) on behalf of the NBU. For the first time it allows Beekeepers to access their own apiary records, diagnostic histories and details over the web.
Beekeepers can register online as a Beekeeper and can request an apiary visit from their local inspector who will provide any help and advice needed. The website also provides information on the functional activities of the NBU, legislation, pests and diseases including their recognition and control, interactive maps, current research areas, publications, advisory leaflets and key contacts.

(This is the most recent information received from the National Bee Unit).

DEPARTMENT OF AGRICULTURE AND RURAL DEVELOPMENT FOR NORTHERN IRELAND

WWW.dardni.gov.uk

BEE ADVISER FOR THE DEPARTMENT
Paul Moore
Agriculture & Food Science Centre Newforge Lane
BELFAST BT9 5PX
028 9025 5288
Fax: 028 9025 5003
E-mail, Paul.J.Moore@dardni.gov.uk

TRAINING COURSES:
Greenmount Campus
College of Agriculture Food and Rural Enterprise:
INFORMATION IS AVAILABLE FROM THE COLLEGE AT
028 9442 6631
Fax: 028 9442 6606
E-mail, Kevin.O'Donnell@dardni.gov.uk

Honeybee Regional Report for Northern Ireland 2007

Bee Health Surveys

Speculation in the media of the threat of CCD to local bees ensured that the Bee Inspectorate had to deal with increased reports of bee losses in the spring. While there is no doubt that bee associations could point to high losses amongst beekeepers often it seemed to be the case that varroa monitoring and control could be greatly improved. Findings of high levels of varroa mites in some of the samples lifted in the autumn for varroacide resistance testing would indicate that this remains the case.

The Bee Inspectorate carried out surveys for American foul brood, European foul brood, Small Hive beetle and Tropilaelaps mite along with sampling of bees for resistance testing of varroa mites. American foul brood outbreaks remained high with twelve apiaries found to have the disease. The outbreaks were in many new areas this year indicating a widespread disease presence. No cases of European foul brood were recorded although a number of hives were checked using the field test kits and laboratory analysis. Surveys continued for Small Hive Beetle and Tropilaelaps mite. Apiaries in the vicinity of ports or fruit importers were targeted for Small Hive Beetle inspections using corriboard shelter traps while apiaries that had imported in the past were selected and hive scrapings examined for Tropilaelaps mite.

Varroa

Submissions have reduced significantly since last year as all of the associations reported positive infestation in their areas. As varroa mite incidence has reached a complete establishment within Northern Ireland, more emphasis was

placed on advice on treatment applications and associated resistance monitoring. As in 2006, monitoring was directed at areas of early varroa establishment. Two previous apiaries displaying resistance to treatment had their colonies replaced and no indication of varroacide resistance was recorded.

Again this year more associations are investigating alternative varroa treatments as part of a pest management strategy.

Adult Bee Disease Diagnostics

Acarine and Nosema are both still in evidence although only low numbers of samples were received this year. Concern perhaps was directed to the overall loss of bees and no bodies to submit for analysis.

Residue Sampling

Honey samples were again lifted this year for testing for residues of veterinary medicines and environmental contaminants. Samples lifted last year were found to be satisfactory.

Imports

Thirty-one imports were notified to DARD and a number of follow-up inspections were carried out to check the records and health certificates. These imports came from Greece and Denmark. In some cases health certificates aren't accompanying bees and also notification by beekeepers isn't being carried out. One such incident was raised with the relevant authorities.

The Bee Diseases and Pests Control Order (Northern Ireland) 2007

The above Order came into operation on the 21st May 2007, which brought our list of notifiable pests and diseases into line with England and Wales. Work has started on the Bee Health contingency plan and it is hoped to have a draft of this ready to go to the various bee organisations in February 2008 for consultation.

Thomas Williamson
Senior Bee Inspector DARD
Paul Moore
Bee Disease Diagnostics AFBI
Seamus Hughes
Farm Policy Branch, DARD

THE SCOTTISH GOVERNMENT RURAL PAYMENTS AND INSPECTIONS DIRECTORATE BEE INSPECTORS

HEADQUARTERS
Lead Bee Inspector
Stephen Sunderland,
P Spur, Saughton House,
Broomhouse Drive,
Edinburgh, EH11 3XD
Tel: 0300 244 6672
e-mail: beesmailbox@
scotland.gsi.gov.uk

The Scottish Government (SG) is responsible for bee health policy in Scotland. SG recognises the importance of a strong bee health programme, not only for the production of honey, but also for the contribution that bees make to the pollination of many crop species and to the wider environment.

Honeybees are susceptible to a variety of threats, including pests and diseases, the likelihood and consequences of which have increased significantly over the last few years. The Scottish Government takes very seriously any biosecurity threat to the sustainability of the apiculture sector and is working closely with colleagues in Food and Environment Research Agency's (Fera) National Bee Unit (NBU) to enable a more joined up approach to be taken throughout Great Britain on the issues surrounding bee health.

The Scottish Government has invested in the NBU's national web based database for beekeepers "BeeBase" and actively encourages beekeepers to register onto the system. This service will provide bee health and disease outbreak information and will also assist Bee Inspectors in disease control. BeeBase also provides information on legislation, pests and disease recognition and control, interactive maps, current research areas and key contacts.

Beekeepers have a significant role to play in ensuring disease management and control within their own apiaries are in order as they have a legal obligation to report any suspicion of a notifiable disease or pest to the Bee Inspector at their local Scottish Government Rural Payments Inspections Directorate (SGRPID) Area Office.

The Bee Inspectors, based at Area Offices of SGRPID, are responsible for the operation of The Bee Diseases and Pests

Control (Scotland) Order 2007 in their area with duties including:-

- inspection of apiaries for presence of statutory bee diseases
- taking and delivering samples to SASA,
- issuing and removal of 'Standstill Notices'
- issuing of 'Destruction Notices' and supervising destruction
- informing beekeepers of treatment options for European Foul Brood (EFB), where appropriate
- granting the option, after taking account of the recommendations of SASA, and carrying out treatment
- carrying out follow-up inspections after destruction or treatment

SASA

Science and Advice for Scottish Agriculture (SASA) is responsible for providing specialist technical support and is authorised under The Bee Diseases and Pests Control (Scotland) Order 2007 as "SASA". Duties include:

- examination of submitted samples suspected of being infected with American Foul Brood, European Foul Brood, Small Hive Beetle (SHB) or *Tropilaelaps.*
- reporting results on which pathogen or pest is present
- recommending, in consultation with the Bee Inspector, the most suitable option, destruction or treatment, for each individual case of EFB.
- where treatment is agreed, ordering supplies of the approved antibiotic
- provision of a free diagnostic service to beekeepers to identify and confirm presence of varroa.
- maintaining technical liaison with National Bee Unit, The Food and Environment Research Agency, Sand Hutton, York, providing technical documentation as required
- providing training courses and demonstration material as required

SASA (SCIENCE AND ADVICE FOR SCOTTISH AGRICULTURE)
1 Roddinglaw Rd,
Edinburgh, EH12 9FJ
BEE DISEASES,
FIONA HIGHET
Plant Health Section
(0131) 244 8817
PESTICIDE INCIDENTS,
ELIZABETH SHARP
Chemistry Section
(0131) 244 8874

PESTICIDE INCIDENTS

As part of the Wildlife Incident Investigation Scheme, SASA undertakes analytical investigations into bee mortalities where pesticide poisoning may have been involved. Beekeepers should send samples of dead bees (200) direct to SASA, Chemistry Section, for analysis. In the case of major incidents, beekeepers are advised to contact their nearest SGRPID Area Office so that an early field investigation can be instigated.

THE FOLLOWING SCOTTISH GOVERNMENT RURAL PAYMENTS AND INSPECTIONS DIRECTORATE (SGRPID) STAFF ARE AUTHORISED BEE INSPECTORS. ALL BEE INSPECTORS HAVE EMAIL ADDRESSES AS "FIRSTNAME.SURNAME@SCOTLAND.GSI.GOV.UK"

SOUTHERN - DUMFRIES AREA OFFICE,
Angus Cameron
161 Brooms Road, Dumfries
DG1 3ES
(01387) 274400
Fax: (01387) 274440

SOUTH EASTERN - GALASHIELS AREA OFFICE,
Angus MacAskill
Cotgreen Road,
Tweedbank, Galashiels,
Scottish Borders, TD1 3SG
(01896) 892400
Fax: (01896) 892424

SOUTH WESTERN - AYR AREA OFFICE,
John Smith
Russell House, King Street,
Ayr, South Ayrshire,
KA8 0BG
(01292) 291300
Fax: (01292) 291301

EDINBURGH (HQ)
Steve Sunderland
P Spur, Saughton House,
Broomhouse Drive,
Edinburgh.
EH11 3XD
0300 244 6672
Fax: 0300 244 9797

GRAMPIAN - INVERURIE AREA OFFICE,
Kirsteen Sutherland
Thainstone Court,
Inverurie, Grampian,
Aberdeenshire, AB51 5YA
(01467) 626247
Fax: (01467) 626217

GRAEME SHARPE, APICULTURE
Specialist, Veterinary
Services, SAC,
Auchincruive, Ayr.
Tel:01292 525375

SCOTTISH AGRICULTURAL COLLEGE (SAC)

The Scottish Government supports a full-time apiculture specialist (Graeme Sharpe) who provides free of charge comprehensive advisory, training and education programmes for beekeepers throughout Scotland on all aspects of Integrated Pest Management and good husbandry including the control of Varroa. Graeme also promotes awareness of notifiable bee diseases and pests and the provision of general advice of good husbandry and management practices to ensure healthy honeybee colonies.

WWW.SCOTLAND.GOV.UK/TOPICS/APICULTURE/GRANTS/INSPECTIONS/BEEINSPECTIONS

USEFUL TABLES

BEEKEEPING METRIC CONVERTION TABLES

°CENT	FAHR
0	32
5	40
7	44
30	86
34	92
38	100
43	110
49	120
54	130
60	140
62	144
82	180
90	194
100	212

INCH	MM
1/25	1
1/12	2
1/8	3
1/16	5
1/4	6
5/16	8
3/8	9
1/2	12.5
5/8	16
3/4	18
7/8	22
1	25
1 1/16	27
1 3/8	35
1 9/20	37
1 1/2	38

INCH	MM
1 5/8	42
1 11/16	43
1 9/20	48
2	51
3	76
4 1/4	108
4 1/2	114
4 3/4	121
5 1/2	140
5 3/4	146
6	152
6 1/4	159
8 1/4	216
8 3/4	223
9 1/8	232
9 3/8	239
9 9/16	246

INCH	MM
10	254
10 1/4	260
11 1/4	286
11 1/2	292
11 3/4	298
12	305
14	356
16 1/4	413
16 1/2	49
17	431
17 5/8	448
18 1/8	460
18 1/4	483
20	508
21 1/2	546
21 3/4	552
22	559

INTERNATIONAL QUEEN MARKING COLOURS

YEAR ENDING	COLOUR	REMEMBER
1 & 6	WHITE	Will
2 & 7	YELLOW	You
3 & 8	RED	Raise
4 & 9	GREEN	Good
5 & 0	BLUE	Bees?

USEFUL TABLES

BOTTOM BEE-SPACE HIVES

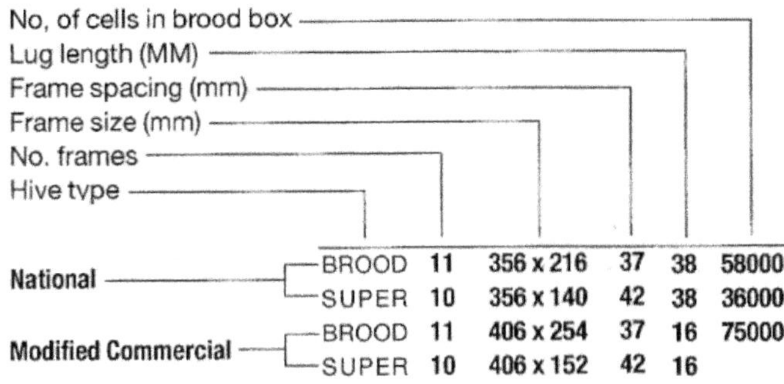

Hive type		No. frames	Frame size (mm)	Frame spacing (mm)	Lug length (MM)	No, of cells in brood box
National	BROOD	11	356 x 216	37	38	58000
	SUPER	10	356 x 140	42	38	36000
Modified Commercial	BROOD	11	406 x 254	37	16	75000
	SUPER	10	406 x 152	42	16	

TOP BEE-SPACE HIVES

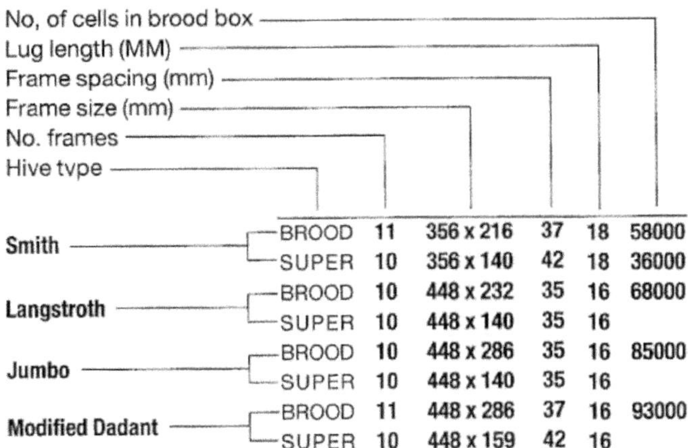

Hive tvpe		No. frames	Frame size (mm)	Frame spacing (mm)	Lug length (MM)	No, of cells in brood box
Smith	BROOD	11	356 x 216	37	18	58000
	SUPER	10	356 x 140	42	18	36000
Langstroth	BROOD	10	448 x 232	35	16	68000
	SUPER	10	448 x 140	35	16	
Jumbo	BROOD	10	448 x 286	35	16	85000
	SUPER	10	448 x 140	35	16	
Modified Dadant	BROOD	11	448 x 286	37	16	93000
	SUPER	10	448 x 159	42	16	

USEFUL TABLES

CONVERSION FACTORS

TEMPERATURE	
Fahrenheit > Celcius (Centigrade)	- 32, x 0.5555 ($^5/_9$)
Celcius > Fahrenheit	x 1.8 ($^9/_5$), + 32

WEIGHT	
Ounces > Pounds	x 28.3495
Pounds > Grams	x 453.59237
Hundredweights > Kilograms	x 50.8
Grams > Ounces	÷ 28.3495
Kilograms > Pounds	x 2.2142

LENGTH	
Inches > Centimetres	x 2.54
Yards > Metres	x 0.9144
Miles > Kilometres	x 1.609
Centimetres > Inches	x 0.3937
Metres > Yards	x 1.0936
Kilometres > Miles	÷ 1.609

AREA	
Acres > Hectares	x 0.404686
Hectares > Acres	x 2.47105

VOLUMN	
Pints > Litres	x 0.5683
Gallons > Litres	x 4.546
Litres > Pints	x 1.7598
Litres > Gallons	x 0.21997

www.ingramcontent.com/pod-product-compliance
Ingram Content Group UK Ltd.
Pitfield, Milton Keynes, MK11 3LW, UK
UKHW021331070726
13610UKWH00011B/31